# Estate Downsizing for Caregivers

## Transitioning from a home to an apartment or care facility

# Estate Downsizing for Caregivers

## Transitioning from a home to an apartment or care facility

Susan Bewsey

**Self-Counsel Press**
*(a division of)*
International Self-Counsel Press Ltd.
USA        Canada

*Self-Counsel Press acknowledges the financial support of the Government of Canada through the Canada Book Fund for our publishing activities.*

*First edition: 2014*

**Library and Archives Canada Cataloguing in Publication**

Bewsey, Susan, author
     Estate downsizing for caregivers : transitioning from a home to an apartment or care facility / Susan Bewsey.

(Eldercare series)
Issued in print and electronic formats.
ISBN 978-1-77040-191-4 (pbk.).—ISBN 978-1-77040-946-0 (epub).— ISBN 978-1-77040-947-7 (kindle)


     1. Moving, Household.  2. Personal belongings.  3. Estate planning. I. Title.  II. Series: Eldercare series

| | | |
|---|---|---|
| TX307.B49 2014 | 648'.9 | C2014-901048-6 |
| | | C2014-901049-4 |

Self-Counsel Press
*(a division of)*
International Self-Counsel Press Ltd.

| | |
|---|---|
| Bellingham, WA | North Vancouver, BC |
| USA | Canada |

Printed in Canada

# Contents

## Questionnaires

# Notice to Readers

Laws are constantly changing. Every effort is made to keep this publication as current as possible. However, the author, the publisher, and the vendor of this book make no representations or warranties regarding the outcome or the use to which the information in this book is put and are not assuming any liability for any claims, losses, or damages arising out of the use of this book. The reader should not rely on the author or the publisher of this book for any professional advice. Please be sure that you have the most recent edition.

# Acknowledgements

With gratitude to the following: Self-Counsel Press for the opportunity and patient support, and for caring to publish for the everyday person; Vancouver Island Health Authority for their support and guidance in caring of the sick, the disabled, the disenfranchised, and the elderly; my family and friends; and to the many invisible caregivers of the world. Thank you.

> *"To the world you may be one person, but to one person, you may be the world."*
>
> — DR. SEUSS/BILL WILSON

# Preface

This book came about because I was downsizing, people around me were downsizing, and we were all looking for help in some fashion. I was inspired by a request to share my experiences and to shift focus from outlining a model of a downsize business to preparing a practical guide for volunteer caregivers and individuals facing these scenarios.

I have included references that assisted me in composing this writing, but realize that many individuals, particularly our more senior elders may not have access to computers. I urge caregivers and others to assist by printing out information that may be of use in having dialogue on downsizing with elders in their care.

I tried to write this simply, practically, and in a positive light. I played music from various eras as I dealt with subjects that sometimes were emotionally challenging to write. I try to bring the reader through the steps involved in downsizing in sequence or chronological order, although at times that is not always possible because events can and do occur at the same time, and we are called upon to put on our juggling hats. I hope that reading this book may offer an oasis of calm in a sea of information when a downsizing situation occurs in your life.

What help we as caregivers are able to provide and receive is changing in a rapidly progressive world. Caregiving now encompasses fields of professional study, licensing, associations, and organizations. Once upon a time it was done for no compensation by family, friends and neighbors, and indeed throughout the world it still is. This guide is intended for the unpaid, unsung heroes who offer their time and energy in support of others.

Downsizing is a routine part of life. We transition from acquiring belongings for many years to the disposition of those very belongings. Although disposing of things may seem a straightforward exercise, downsizing without planning can be a taxing, complicated exercise fraught with challenges and stress. In addition to the physical aspects of contending with sorting, taking inventory, valuing, storing, and disposal of goods, is the emotional and psychological toll taken on all parties involved in seeing a downsize task through to completion all the while attending to the personal needs of individuals.

In my life, I have experienced several sudden downsizings. I was called upon to assist in the transition of elderly individuals as they moved into long-term care; I have helped out in sudden death scenarios; relocated a blind widower and his possessions to his country of birth; and I have helped in a downsizing due to illness and disability. The phone lines burned back and forth as friends offered and shared suggestions and experiences. Although there was writing on the subject in magazines, periodicals, and brochures, I found nothing all under one roof. Guidance and information gathered was often written in difficult to understand context or legalese and was only available to me if I knew to ask for it.

I found little in the way of practical steps to take and when to take them. It was a hard learned lesson a day, or so it seemed. Over the years I have collected and maintained information from many sources in an attempt to piece together a roadmap for when the situation presents itself again.

The writing of this is, in part, because of my desire to share valuable information and lessons learned with a receptive audience, and as a cathartic exercise in seeing downsizing as a positive and inevitable experience.

For individuals with downsizing needs, this guide is intended to assist you in conducting your own downsizing, by assembling a team of help. For individuals who will be assisting others, this guide is intended to provide guidance on how to proceed with decision making. For those in the midst of a career change, this guide may assist you in discovering an employment niche, or a business concept to which you can apply your knowledge and skills.

Please read through the sections that may be appropriate for your situation; use the questionnaires as a guide, write on them, personalize them as needed, print them from the download kit included with this book, and start your own downsizing plans.

# Introduction

## 1. What Is Downsizing?

*Downsize (verb): to make something smaller or to undergo a reduction in size or quantity.*

There is more than one time in our lives when we experience downsizing. We downsize when we leave a childhood home to set up our first apartment for school or for a job in a new locale. We downsize when we may have personally been downsized in our jobs or careers. We downsize when our relationships with others have changed, in partnering, in the dissolution of a partnership, as a result of the passing of a significant other, or to accommodate a friend or family member. We downsize when we grow older and no longer wish to, or are able to maintain our family homes and sometimes we downsize to simplify our lives.

Each time we downsize, we are responding to adjusting physical spaces to suit financial, physical, and emotional needs, or any combination of life-altering circumstances.

According to statistics provided by the governments and organizations of Canada,[1] the United States,[2] the United Kingdom,[3] and Australia,[4] demographic studies reveal that approximately 79 to 100 million people will be retiring and an estimated 10,000 people in North America alone will turn 65 every day for the next 19 years.

This is relevant because the baby boomers, their children, and their parents will be altering living arrangements and adjusting their lives to embrace new normals.

The parents of the baby boomers, aged 71 plus currently — the silent generation — will require accommodations in retirement homes, assisted living residences, or with friends or family. The children of baby boomers, aged 29 to 44 — the Gen X'ers — will make living arrangement changes to accommodate their own migrating families and jobs. Another 100 million movers, the Millennials[5], aged 29 and younger are embarking on establishing their own careers, lifestyles, and families. There is a boomerang generation[6] who return home to care for elderly or disabled family members, or for economic reasons. And there are the lifestyle changes of places and spaces for people living newly single lives by choice or circumstance.

We are coming into an era that is experiencing a boom (or spike upward) in providing caregiving and downsizing services to people in transition. For some, their downsizing projects will be initiated by choice, such as a lifestyle change to minimalize, a planned downsize; for others, it will be as a result of an unexpected circumstance such as illness, financial catastrophe or death, a sudden downsize. If we are fortunate, with good mental and physical health, we will be the architects of our downsizing experiences. We will perform tasks on our own or delegate tasks to service providers or caregivers, both personal and professional. The circumstances will depend on our abilities and preferences at the time, or by the measures we have previously put into place, such as instructions we have formally or legally directed to a lawyer, or a representative such as a relocation advisor, a professional organizer, or downsizing service provider who will be carrying out our wishes by contractual agreement.

In my research, I discovered many gifted writers on the subject. Resources online today are numerous, many more than when I was

---

1 *Census in Brief — Generations in Canada — Age and sex, 2011 Census. http://www12.statcan.gc.ca/census-recensement/2011/as-sa/98-311-x/98-311-x2011003_2-eng.pdf
2 US http://www.pewresearch.org/daily-number/baby-boomers-retire/
3 Population UK. http://www.ons.gov.uk/ons/taxonomy/index.html?nscl=Population#tab-sum-pub
4 australia.gov.au. Baby Boomers-http://australia.gov.au/about-australia/australian-story/baby-boomers
5 http://www.pewsocialtrends.org/2012/03/15/the-boomerang-generation/
6 http://www.pewresearch.org/2009/12/10/the-millennials/

caregiving and downsizing for others a few short years ago. Availability of information on the subject has increased, including in-depth information respecting aging and caregiving posted online by governments. I followed URLs and blogs about downsizing, read newspapers published from one coast to the other, scanned and clipped magazine articles, and continued to collect brochures and informative literature. I discovered that downsizing and caregiving were beginning to be featured on a regular basis.

I discovered many businesses evolving to meet the growing demand for downsizing assistance by aging and transitioning people. From small towns to large urban centers, entrepreneurial, service-minded individuals were offering downsizing services. Some models were very efficient and professional, while others were evolving in their quest to find an employment niche in a growing downsizing marketplace. The one message that remained consistent was that there is an ever-growing need for help and a growing shortage of helpers.

## 2. Who Are the Caregivers?

Almost every one of us will provide some form of caregiving in our lives. Some people will be trained and employed in specific fields of caregiving, but most will be everyday people who volunteer their time to help friends, family members, and neighbors.

A caregiver is defined by Merriam Webster dictionary as "a person who gives help and protection to someone (such as a child, an old person, or someone who is sick," or "a person who provides direct care (as for children, elderly people, the disabled or the chronically ill."

There are live-in caregivers, companion caregivers, and family caregivers to name a few possibilities.

Caregivers provide support and care to reduce the suffering of another, and assist in coping and functioning. Caregiving can reduce the financial burden on families and governments, often to the detriment of the caregivers' own well-being. Caregivers tend to be empathic individuals; they may also be professional individuals who possess the skills, training, and accreditation to provide support within a defined job description.

The characteristics of a caregiver may be defined simply by looking into your mirror.

This book and the exercises herein were created for the individual and the nonprofessional caregiver (volunteer) who needs to downsize personally or for another person.

Some interesting statistics I discovered while researching caregivers: A 2001 census in the UK revealed that 6 million or more people provided unpaid care for a relative, friend, or neighbor and at least one third of all people will be providing care to another in their lifetime. Further, more than 175,000 caregivers are under the age of 18. Italy has the highest percentage of people aged 65 or older. More than 1.5 million people under the age of 25 in Australia are facing care responsibilities for an elderly or disabled person. More than 10 million people are needed to provide care today to an aging population in China. And in the US, 43.5 million adult family caregivers care for someone aged 50 and older and 61.6 million people have provided unpaid care to another in the recent past.

Unpaid caregiving provided by volunteer and family members saves governments billions of dollars annually in providing care for the elderly and the disabled; it eases stress on the health system and the support of caregivers is encouraged to continue.

This altruism and responsibility however comes at a cost to the caregiver in the toll it takes on them physically, mentally, emotionally, and financially; indeed there is a term for it, it is called "caregiver burnout" and individuals are encouraged to read up on the subject. Precautionary measures, such as learning to deal effectively with the downsizing of our estates, as well as how to protect our health, will help to ensure our own well-being and the well-being of those of will be tasked with our care.

## 3. Who Downsizes?

Who downsizes and for whom?

- Self.
- Spouse for spouse.
- Children for parents.
- Children for grandparents.
- Caregivers for the elderly or the disabled.
- Trustee/guardian/executor for those under care.
- Parents for children.
- Sibling for sibling.
- Friends for others.
- Legal representatives.

- Arm's length individuals.
- Strangers / advocates.
- Community workers for clients.
- Moving and downsizing companies for clients.
- Employees for employers.
- Other.

When does downsizing occur?

- Moving away to a school or job.
- Moving in with a roommate.
- Moving into a smaller home.
- During renovations/temporarily.
- Moving in with family.
- Moving to a care facility.
- After an illness.
- After a death.

For which of the above situation(s) do you feel you need to prepare yourself?

Will you be doing the downsizing alone from start to finish, or will you have help? If you have done this before, what will you do differently this time? Why?

## 4. What Do We Downsize?

When downsizing, we reduce our belongings, homes, cottages, vehicles, books, artwork, music, clothing, jewelry, toys, tools, stuff, real estate, intellectual property, money, investments, things we own that we purchased, inherited, acquired, built or created can be used to define our economic standing in a community, showcase our interests and hobbies, for investment purposes, and for sentiment.

We are coming into the greatest trade-off of our belongings in history and the resulting trillions of dollars to baby boomer heirs and beneficiaries.

Our belongings make up some of that hand-over.

# 5. A Little History: How Has Downsizing Changed?

We have great grandparents, grandparents, uncles, aunts, and parents; sometimes two sets of families or friends, or more, living and passing on histories and belongings. These are our elders.

In the past things were passed down from generation to generation and family members or close friends attended to wrapping up the affairs of the elderly and distributing belongings, as directed verbally, or as they saw fit.

A look at Table 1 may you give an idea of some of the events our elders have seen, heard and experienced as life was humming along waiting for us to grow older.

When the baby boomers were young and in the acquiring stages of life, belongings came from various sources. Some things were purchased and other items were acquired by inheritances. Think about the excitement of finding a vintage vehicle intact under a tarp in Grandfather's barn, or heirlooms still packed in trunks from a journey across oceans by immigrating families who left homes and family to make their way in newer worlds.

Once there were door-to-door salesmen selling wares, and items were purchased from mail-order catalogues. Before Google and countless other free online search engines, knowledge and facts were gleaned from the likes of the *Encyclopedia Britannica* which was distributed by salesmen who carted leather satchels, heavy with bound tomes, to suburban homes. Fuller Brush knocked on doors to promote cleaning brushes and products to follow up after the diminishing industry of cleaning military brushes when the war ended. Avon encouraged women to become independent businesspeople by utilizing their socializing and networking skills with other women. It was a time of growing consumerism. Prior to this, to survive the Depression, people traded and shared goods and homes, repaired things, and goods were recycled; to think that once, people would use catalogues as toilet paper! Items that were sale worthy were often exchanged for food or donated to the less fortunate as few were buying anything in the Depression era. People owned less and were frugal. People became great savers and as a result their children became inheritors of their belongings.

The world changed after the two World Wars. Returning servicemen were required to focus on rebuilding their lives, families, and communities. In the mid 1940s, the baby boom commenced. Babies were born in record numbers, houses were built, industries were established, and employment was booming along with industry growth.

The average size of a middle-class suburban house in 1950 was typically under 1,000 square feet with two or three bedrooms and one (perhaps one and a half) bathroom(s).

Yards were large and landscaped. Lawns were cut with push mowers. There was a stay-at-home parent, often the mom, a black and white television with a limited number or channels that were broadcast for a limited time each day. People planted vegetable gardens and fruit trees. Fortunate families had one car. Tract houses were built close to industry and factories to meet housing demands during housing shortages, and until such time as the construction industry and incomes provision could catch up. The concept of mortgages was expanded to more people, for larger homes and growing families. Clothing was washed in wringer washing machines and hung on clotheslines to dry, and was ironed and mended. Sewing machines and sewing kits were a staple. People had daily chores to maintain their homes and families and meals were cooked three times or more daily. Milk and mail were delivered to the door, and bread was homemade or purchased fresh from local bakeries. Few people had vacuum cleaners; floors were swept, handwashed, and waxed with paste wax.

People listened to radios as a family activity, and once a week, maybe would go to an afternoon movie. The extravagant cost of a movie and popcorn was 10 to 25 cents depending on the movie house.

Handkerchiefs were used compared to disposable tissues today, and microwaves were the stuff of science fiction movies. Those who acquired the luxury of a telephone used an operator to dial, or had to wait until another party freed up space on telephone lines so they could make a call (or listen in on others' conversations, as party lines were de rigueur).

Often, grandmas and grandpas could be found living with their adult children, still contributing to the family. In familiar surroundings they were indulged by their expanding families, cooking, using tools and adding colorful stories to family dinners. Many of these elder generations were immigrants who had fled their native countries following the war to start a new life. What they owned or brought from their past such as framed photos, books, Bibles, wedding dresses, and tools were stored in trunks in their rooms, or attics, and had to be shipped by sea, or brought with them on the voyage to a new world. Often there was a hushed and respectful indulgence to aging memories and bodies given health appropriate tasks to accommodate their need to be needed and contribute. Children would learn from this scenario that there were many generations in a family and different stages to accommodate, endure and live in close proximity to. There was respect and tolerance offered. Our elders then were not the invisible ones.

The rebellious youth (perhaps now known as your parents or grandparents) as teenagers were discovering music, poodle skirts, the drive-in restaurant, and rock and roll. These are our baby boomers.

Fast forward to today, homes have more than doubled in size, and hardly a granny or grandpa is to be found on the premises. Farms have become suburbs and cities with all the amenities associated; day-to-day living seems to go at a very fast pace. We have acquired more over the years through purchasing and inheritance, and we are now facing what best to do with the belongings as we face our own downsize situations in a very fast and disposable world.

What are we acquiring now? How and why? Can you fill in the blanks in Table 1?

Yes, the world has changed and, in many ways, despite the increase in population it has become more diverse and a little less mysterious. Travel, both physical and virtual, has allowed us embrace more cultures and experience more styles. It is easier to understand and acquire the exotic as well as the common as we are able to acquire belongings from different places and peoples. There is a greater compilation of history from many sources such as family biographies and genealogy. We now have the added benefit of documenting our lives online for select audiences or larger audiences, for private sharing or for public sharing. Household luxuries we acquired on our independent journeys are now sought by others on journeys toward making their own new homes.

As you prepare to research the values of your soon-to-be-downsized belongings, you are advised to consider the era and uses of those things and what is nostalgic about them which could result in them being more sought after. What is your motivation as you pass along your belongings, your history? What memories will you be marketing? What sentiment are you selling or donating? Who can afford it and who wants it?

As you think about distributing your belongings, you might consider where they came from and their nostalgic value to you or possibly to others. Were they:

- Inherited?
- Collected?

Table 1
## POSSESSIONS THEN AND NOW

| Era | What did we acquire? | Top music and books | Top news story and celebrity |
|---|---|---|---|
| 1940's persons now aged 70+ | • land<br>• tailored clothing, hats, gloves<br>• a car<br>• furniture<br>• china<br>• typewriters<br>• records (78 rpm)<br>• magazines<br>• cigarettes<br>• small appliances<br>• musical instruments<br>• toys | • swing music<br>• bobby socks<br>• Benny Goodman<br>• Glenn Miller<br>• Jimmy Dorsey<br>• Bing Crosby<br>• Frank Sinatra<br>• "I'll never smile again"<br>• "I Love You for Sentimental Reasons" | • Pearl Harbor<br>• Anne Frank<br>• D Day<br>• Hiroshima<br>• Bikinis |
| 1950's persons now aged 60+ | • houses, bungalows<br>• furniture<br>• larger appliances<br>• toasters, mix masters<br>• jewelry<br>• party clothes, knee length skirts<br>• sports cards<br>• sunglasses<br>• fashionable things<br>• perfumes<br>• sewing machines<br>• stamp collections<br>• toy collections<br>• records (45 rpm)<br>• black and white TV's | • Rock and roll<br>• Elvis Presley<br>• McGuire Sisters<br>• Fats Domino<br>• Rosemary Clooney<br>• Duke Ellington<br>• Ray Charles<br>• Doris Day<br>• Everly Brothers<br>• Dinah Shore<br>• Peggy Lee<br>• "Johnny Be Good"<br>• "Heartbreak Hotel"<br>• "Rock Around the Clock" | • credit cards<br>• Korean War<br>• colour television<br>• seat belts<br>• Queen Elizabeth<br>• polio vaccine<br>• first Playboy<br>• Disneyland<br>• hula hoops<br>• Lego<br>• NASA<br>• peace symbol |

| | | | |
|---|---|---|---|
| 1960's persons now aged 50+ | • telephones<br>• jewelry<br>• birth control<br>• colour televisions<br>• records (the LP)<br>• fancier appliances<br>• bigger cars<br>• cameras<br>• packaged food and treats<br>• wall to wall carpets<br>• mono shirts<br>• toaster and microwave ovens<br>• GI Joes and Barbies<br>• instant coffee<br>• blue jeans<br>• macrame | • Beatles<br>• Supremes<br>• Bee Gees<br>• Cream<br>• Del Shannon<br>• Bob Dylan<br>• Rolling Stones<br>• Beach Boys<br>• Jim Hendrix<br>• Led Zeppelin<br>• CCR<br>• The Weight | • birth control pill<br>• man on the moon<br>• first James Bond movie<br>• Marilyn Monroe's death<br>• Kennedy assassinations<br>• Nelson Mandel imprisoned<br>• Star Trek<br>• Sesame Street<br>• ARPAnet (1st internet) created |
| 1970's persons now aged 40+ | | | |
| 1980's persons now aged 30+ | | | |
| 1990's persons now aged 20+ | | | |
| What are we buying now? | | | |

- Purchased?
- Built?

## 6. Downsizing Considerations

Before you plan to move or embark on a downsize project, give thought to your personal situation as it is and how it will be and what time frame you are considering.

- Is there an urgency to the downsize you are considering?
- What are the time constraints?
- What are the physical constraints?
- Is achieving value for your belongings necessary to fund a relocation or other expense?
- Is preserving history of items of significance to you or another?
- Are there other issues about your possessions that need to be considered?
- Is there a need or want to replace belongings?
- Will you be hiring, subcontracting, or using professional downsize services?
- Will you be getting assistance from volunteers, friends, or neighbors?
- What repairs are needed?
- What storage is needed?
- What disposal arrangements are needed?
- Do you have outstanding authorities, or legalities such as contracts or powers of attorney to attend to?
- What government notifications, trustees, or guardians will be required, if any?
- Will you need new insurance, nursing, or security services?
- Do you have to transfer extended warranties or transferable service contracts?
- If you are leaving an empty house, do you require vacancy permits?
- If you are conducting sales, do you require business licenses?
- What are your charitable and philanthropic considerations?

- Will you need to make arrangements for accounting, such as tax returns and change of status, record storage?
- If you are selling your possessions, what advertising and notices will you need?
- Do you have any issues with respect to chemical disposition and permits?
- Can you perform, or have help in researching lawyers, accountants, real estate agents, auction houses, technical support, etc.?
- What will your transportation needs be?
- Are there any landscaping or plants you want to keep or donate?
- Pets: will they accompany you on your journey, or will they need new homes?
- Do you have subscriptions that will need canceling or redirecting?
- Will you have cable or satellite, and a landline or a cellular phone?

Also give thought to everyday personal services to which you are accustomed and will need to replace if you move away such as:

- Hairdresser.
- Veterinarian.
- Physiotherapist.
- Coffee shop.
- Repair shops.
- Physician.
- Lawyer.
- Accountant.
- Recreation centers.
- Hobby clubs.
- Familiar places.
- Familiar faces.
- Support networks.

# 7. Downsizing Flow, from Start to Finish

Simplified, a downsizing follows this path.

- Know yourself or the individual for whom you are downsizing. (Complete the Know Yourself questionnaire in Chapter 4.)
- Know your team or that individual's team.
- Research (places and things).
- Set a goal.
- Reinforce the goal with an action or mission statement.
- Make plans (utilize the who, what, where, when and how format).
- Identify priorities.
- Make to-do lists and schedule tasks.
- Take stock and inventory.
- Commence the downsizing plan (also referred to as a personal succession plan).
- Take the task through to completion.
- Keep perspective.
- Make decisions about what to do with belongings.
- Revisit and revise plans as needed.
- Get and give help (delegate if needed).
- Attend to needs.
- Communicate.
- Obtain feedback on progress.
- Troubleshoot as needed.

The following chapters will cover the above in more detail for both the individual and the caregiver.

# 8. Putting Together Your Downsizing Team

The following is an initial list of the people with whom you should consult with and from whom you should request advice. They are the advisors who will make up your team and are your support network. For some, a fee will be required, and for others they will be compensated by the work generated if any.

They may include, but are not limited to, a number of professionals. There is more about team members in Chapter 4 (Human Resources) and Chapter 7 (Service Providers, Caregivers, and Advisors):

- Lawyers.
- Accountants.
- Financial advisors.
- Physician.
- Veterinarians.
- Bankers.
- Realtors.
- Counselors/spiritual advisors/community workers.
- Realtors.
- Home insurers.
- Caregivers.
- Storage companies.
- Downsizing companies.

If possible, meeting with and selecting team members should occur before it becomes a rushed necessity.

1

# How to Look at Downsizing

A recap: What is downsizing?

- Selling or disposing of excess personal property to make more room or to reduce living space.

- Trading down (as in real estate) in size and quantity.

- Reducing (labor and production and inventory) as in business.

- Streamlining, diminishing, downscaling, lessening, lowering, reducing, compressing, condensing, contracting, abbreviating, paring, pruning, shortening, trimming, minimizing, moderating.

- Modifying lifestyle to embrace a reduced income or space or to accommodate health and well-being.

What is downsizing to you? Why?

Table 2 shows the results of a short survey I conducted wherein I asked people what downsizing meant to them. Here are the following reactions at the mention of downsizing.

Table 2

## SHARED REACTIONS FROM PEOPLE WHEN ASKED THEIR THOUGHTS ON DOWNSIZING

| Name | Age | Why? |
|------|-----|------|
| Sandra | 63 | scared about things lost or missed in the future — a loss |
| Catherine | 58 | living simpler, moving to warmer climate |
| Donald | 65 | less work more leisure time |
| Michael | 64 | moving, horrors of reduced income and lifestyle |
| Rhea | 49 | many life changes, simplify life in future |
| Walter | 63 | layoffs, retirement, move nervousness |
| Gail | 58 | reducing to what you can afford |
| Suzanne | 49 | preparation and evolution to a more streamlined life |
| Jack | 60 | sad memories and lots of work cleaning things up |
| Sara | 30 | moving and getting rid of stuff |
| Matt | 30 | getting rid of stuff, reducing manpower |
| Joseph | 50 | house to condo, freedom of attachment to the past |
| Jill | 33 | freedom to travel and explore |
| Elaine | 70 | mobility to freely visit and stay with family |
| Karen | 55 | reducing, whatever, nothing emotional about it |
| Joanne | 49 | liquidation for retirement income |
| Carolyn | 60 | relief, enjoyment of the freedom from attachment |

# 1. Opportunities in Downsizing

Downsizing means to make smaller or reduce, but to the businesses in Table 3, it represents an increase in work and revenues.

For each of the scenarios, the act of downsizing may present a fear or uncertainty to the downsizing individual, but can translate to increased work activity and income to be generated by those providing counsel and services to a marketplace of millions of people in transition.

Table 3

## OPPORTUNITIES IN DOWNSIZING

| Downsizing means | Pros | Cons |
|---|---|---|
| To a lawyer | income | detailed work |
| To an accountant | income | summary work |
| To a financial advisor | income | rebalancing work |
| To a realtor | income | buy and sell |
| To a home insurer | income | |
| To a guidance counselor | income and ability to give respected attention / advice | wrong guidance for individual |
| To a downsize provider or care giver | income | labour, valuation |
| To a company | income for shareholders | reduced wages for labour |
| To a Technical Person | income for instructing, designing scenarios | Challenges with dated equipment, knowledge of clients |
| To a writer | income for biographical projects | |
| To a photographer | income for photographic projects | |
| Other: | | |

Downsizing is a generator of employment so it can be embraced with a positive frame of mind. Downsizing is a good opportunity for establishing and growing new businesses and offering better, needed services.

## 2. Downsizing as a Positive Experience

Making letting go of belongings positive, or meaningful, can help ease the transition for people going through downsizing. There are many ways to make letting go of belongings in a downsizing situation more meaningful.

For some, downsizing is an opportunity to remember, reflect upon, and revisit old memories.

- Consider donating items to organizations that take care of the less fortunate such as Goodwill and Salvation Army.
- Consider donating to a charitable organization such as the SPCA for fundraising.
- Recycle.
- Repurpose: Adapt for a different use.
- Sell old and buy new.
- Gift to friends or family.

If you need inspiration for how to go about these things, consider:

- Walking around furniture stores, observing emerging trends in style and design.
- Scanning newspapers, journals, and magazines; think fashion, furniture, and home decor sections.
- Visiting consignment shops to see what others are downsizing.
- Visiting Goodwill and Salvation Army outlets to see what has been donated.
- Visiting a nursing home to see how life there is lived.

Although the following chapters and situations may not apply to you directly, you may be called upon to assist someone in downsizing in any of these situations. I recommended reading through the whole book, and formulating your own downsizing plan based on the information provided and from questions that may arise as a result of reading.

We don't know what we don't know, so questions are best addressed at the onset of a project.

# 2

# Downsizing Types and Scenarios

On a life lived to 80 years of age, we are youth for the first 20, adults for the next 40, and elders for the balance of our days.

We will make decisions in our youth that will be with us for a very long time. Establishing goals and objectives and making plans should commence as soon as we become adults.

The following sections will cover some of the life events that will trigger downsizing scenarios.

We are faced with two scenarios that will govern our actions and how we take action. In one, we accept that downsizing is a normal part of life and prepare for it as we do any other estate planning. In the other, we find ourselves having to suddenly go into downsize mode and rush through all the steps in moving from attending to the storing and the selling of belongings.

## 1. Planned Downsizing

A planned downsize is an ideal scenario, where we have months or years to prepare.

The downsizing may be discussed and planned with family, friends, and advisors. There will be the added luxury of being able to choose help, research and assign values to goods, and decide whether there are people you wish to reward with gifts.

The planned downsizing may simply take the form of an annual or semi-annual cleanout over a few years or seasons.

Questionnaire 1
## PLANNED OR SUDDEN DOWNSIZING?

Date:

What is creating the downsize need?

How much time do you have to accomplish this task? Why?

How long should this take, ideally?

What do you consider planned?

Why is this a planned downsize?

How long can you work daily?

What are your challenges?

What are your strengths?

Other:

## 2. Sudden Downsizing

The phone rings, a job is offered, a school accepts your application, or a health issue or sudden death triggers the need for either a temporary or a permanent move. This type of situation has unknowns attached to it, and a great deal of stress. Will there be a return to a family home following an illness, or will a surviving spouse require support and alternative care arrangements? Will a job offer be a temporary situation or is there a possibility for a long-term career commitment?

This may be exciting news or a turn of events, or it may be a sudden, sad detour in your life. Even with a happy move, a relocation of your possessions will require some downsizing thought and plans for storage and moving. However, for this writing, a sudden downsizing as a result of illness, injury, or death is the subject that will be covered.

Making decisions while in a state of shock (or grief) is not recommended. Having a downsize plan already thought through and at the ready is recommended. One will then more easily be able to retrieve a plan (from his or her files) and commence, or pass it to someone else to carry out.

In sharing downsize experiences with others, I have heard things such as, "I was rushed, had no help, so I made decisions to dispose of belongings that I wish I would have kept or sold for better value," and "I committed to selling and buying when I should have waited and leased."

The first thing should be to think about these issues, away from the area of the project. Go to a neutral place such as a library, a friend's home, or even an empty room or uncluttered space in the house. Set up a time to sit with a note taking pad of paper. Date the paper and start writing a to-do list. Double or triple space it, because the list will grow.

Not only will the mind and body be taxed with thoughts of physically moving, but also of immediate needs (arranging moving trucks, finding accommodation, making meals, personal adjustments), but there will also be the overwhelming task of contending with current living conditions.

Using physical distance to focus on only a to-do list is so important (as are deep breathing and stretching exercises). Where do you think most clearly? On a walk, in the park, in the morning, at noon, or night? Know this part of yourself and then get started on your lists.

Can you do this in the time allotted or do you need and can you obtain help from volunteers, or will you need to use a downsizing service provider?

When faced with a sudden downsizing situation, and you have not made a downsize plan previously, and you are rushed, take these initial steps:

- Take out a pen and paper.
- Set a goal.
- Write down what you need to do to achieve that goal.
- Estimate the time needed to achieve the tasks that will achieve that goal.
- Estimate the funds available for hiring help, if any.
- Make to-do lists.
- Accomplish one thing at a time, and then move on to another and another.

- Keep a record of your progress.

- Use the checklists from this book if needed and modify them to suit your situation (they are available on the download kit included with this book).

- Ask for and use help. Delegate.

A landlord may have triggered a notice to vacate the premises for a hospitalized tenant, or the premise is depreciating (think, food spoiling in a fridge) and it needs immediate attention, or adverse weather conditions call for a securing of the home, shovelling snow, heat or water issues, or a pet requires alternative care.

You need to consider the following:

1. Do you have legal authority to deal with this situation. For example, are you a legal next of kin? Is there a power of attorney in place? Is there a lawyer, accountant, or financial advisor who knows the affairs of the individual? Is there a trustee or executor (or executrix) appointed who can direct the estate? If so, will they meet with you?

2. Are you aware of any family or asset conflicts? If so seek legal advice on the best way to proceed, before proceeding if possible.

3. Will you need the assistance of a public trustee or public guardian in order to act on assets in peril (or weather, pests, rodents and so on) until legal authority is established?

4. Once you have established authority to act and this has to be a priority, you can proceed. It is recommended that you contact a lawyer or solicitor immediately and take instruction or direction from him or her as to how to best proceed. The family lawyer would be a bonus if there is one.

5. Do not ignore or abandon the living individuals who may have fallen ill. Meet with them in the hospital or nursing home to see them and provide calming assurances at a frightful time in their lives. Let them know you will help in the ways you can so they can be more peaceful and less stressed. Ask them questions, if possible, as to their legal situation, next of kin, and legal representatives. If the individual is unable to communicate, there may be a living will direction with the hospital, physician etc and a lawyer's name affixed or associated with it that you can contact for further guidance and instruction.

6. You may need accommodation in the case of an out of town situation or for convenience. If it is approved by the solicitor,

executor (or executrix) or guardian, you should phone and ask first and the premises is secure and a healthy environment for you. You can use that as your base to visit the individual, while making arrangements to move them into a care facility or to make funeral arrangements if needed and to commence to-do lists, inventory taking, and dealing with packing and downsizing their belongings.

7. When you are speaking with a lawyer or legal representative (if you are not the executor (or executrix) or hold a power of attorney (for example), advise them of:

   a. Why you were notified to assist.

   b. Who notified you.

   c. What the urgency is (an eviction of infirm tenant) or assets in peril or jeopardy of dam-age) including the time constraint.

   d. What your relationship to the individual is.

   e. What permissions you have and in what form.

   f. What permissions you need and from whom.

Be aware that there will be costs involved. Ask for an idea of the costs at the onset, and who will be responsible for paying them and if there will be any reimbursement. Keep a list of all expenses together with receipts. This includes travel, telephone costs, and so on.

When obtaining quotes for service providers such as a downsizing company, try to obtain more than one quote, three being a good number to compare value for services. The same for storage facilities (in the event of probate scenarios or to allow time to take an inventory if an immediate vacancy needs to be effected or simply to allow time to digest and conduct the downsizing effectively).

If you have the authorization and the financial means, you may call a downsizing company, obtain their contract details and also their payment requirements to help you make the decision as to the viability of using their services. Meet with representatives and provide the authority for them to proceed if you are able to do so.

A search online for "downsize, relocation, transition and seniors" may yield results to help you find downsizing companies. It is a recently organized and emerging industry. Some individuals and companies are advertising in seniors' magazines, such as http://www. seniorlivingmag.com/magazine and organizations offering training and designations such as http://www.crtscertification.com will provide referrals to individuals and companies by area, as well as professional organizers: http://www.organizersincanada.com about. Many of these companies list their codes of ethics which are well worth a read.

Many downsizers are individuals operating on a referral basis from previous jobs performed and via lawyers and community support organizations. They have networked with organizations such as local health authorities, hospices, and estate lawyers to introduce their services and are not highly visible in advertising en masse, but a call to them will reveal how busy they are. I encourage individuals to make contact and appointments to meet with downsize services ahead of the need.

Quite often downsizing is thought to be from larger home to a smaller home when in fact it can also be within our own homes when space is needed to accommodate other people, such as an ill family member or friend. Downsizing is not just for people going into nursing homes.

Here are a few examples:

- Attending higher education, going away to colleges.
- Moving for employment or self employment opportunities.
- Marriage and partnering.
- Growing families.
- Taking career sabbaticals.
- Desire to move to better climates.
- Economic cutbacks or bankruptcy.
- Minimalizing to a simpler lifestyle.
- Empty nesting.
- Retirement.
- Divorce.
- Death.
- Accommodating individuals living with illness or disability.
- Volunteering in organizations that help transitioning people in need.
- Assisting following a catastrophe, such as after a fire or building issue.

## 2.1 Downsizing for empty nesters

The family has grown and are moving along in life to colleges, jobs and careers, and partnerships. An empty nester is a parent or parents whose children have moved away from home.

What now? You look around the house and it's suddenly much quieter and much larger than you may want, need or can afford. Perhaps you are considering taking up art classes, yoga, or going back for an advanced degree. You are starting to exhale a little. You wonder if it isn't too soon to start thinking about downsizing?

A planned downsize for empty nesters can commence as early as when teens or older children are in the final year of high school or when the child announces his or her intention to move or depart. Empty nesters have the large task of dealing not only with their own belongings, but also with the belongings of children who have left. There are the questions of what to keep for sentimental reasons or practical reasons. This will also include the task of redecorating vacated rooms after a departed family member. Should it be a permanent redecoration? What if the student returns home and needs a room to stay in? Will the room possibly be used for housing an elderly relative? The planning for this can be taxing. This can also be a sad time for parents who have made children their focus; the sudden loss of the child in the house can cause depression and anxiety as parents refocus on new ways to fill their hours, shop for meals, and keep in touch with distant children. For others, they may be counting the days until the youngster flies the nest.

Plan ahead, make a wish list, give yourself time to adjust (a year or more), find a support group, rethink your routine, where and how to grocery shop, exercise, what to do with extra time and space. Will you redecorate? Will you will use the space vacated as a hobby room, for example, or perhaps will you rent it out to other students? Talk to others who have done this and compare their experience with yours to decide how this will work for you.

To-Dos:

- Make a wish list of what you would like to do, where you want to live and how you would like your life to be now that the nest is emptied.

- Give yourself time to adjust (a year or more).

- Join a support group in your community or online of other empty nesters.

- Rethink and refashion your routine,( where and how to grocery shop, exercise, what to do with extra time and space, and in some cases money).

- Redecorate to accommodate new lifestyle and changes.

- Reinvent the space vacated by family to a hobby room.

- Rent it out for company or additional revenue.

## Questionnaire 2
## QUESTIONS TO ASK OF DEPARTING CHILDREN BY THE (SOON-TO-BE) EMPTY NESTER

Date:

What is the anticipated vacate date?

Is this a permanent or semi-permanent departure?

Will the young adult be taking furniture?

What furniture will be required?

Will shipping be needed?

Will the move be to shared accommodation?

Will storage be provided?

When do they plan their first return visit?

Will they require tenant insurance?

When will your first visit to them be?

What does the exiting young adults want to do with their remaining things?

Will they participate in the sorting?

Will they participate in the packing?

What means of communication will you be using to remain in contact?

How often will you communicate (weekly, monthly, etc.)?

Do you have insurance policies that require adjustments?

Do you have investment or banking arrangements that require authorization or other adjustments?

Are there medical issues that require attention?

Is there an anticipated return date?

Other:

### 2.1a Downsizing for empty nesters when adult children return home

Adult children may move back home due to finances, health, or other factors. To obtain better knowledge of what is to be faced, empty nesters should ask questions. Use your own words and frame the questions to suit the situation.

Questionnaire 3
## QUESTIONS TO ASK RETURNING CHILDREN BY EMPTY NESTERS

Date:

When are you returning?

How long do you think you will be here?

Will you be bringing anyone with you?

Will you be bringing furniture?

How much space will you need?

Will you be bringing a pet?

Do you have a source of income?

Will you need medical care or other treatment?

What are your expectations of me (us) and what help are you needing?

Is there any other support you will need?

Other:

## 2.2 Downsizing for retirees

For our purposes, we will consider a retiree to be an individual who has ceased full-time work due to an age limit, the end of a contractual obligation, or due to a disability.

After a lifetime of contributing and weathering life's challenges, the slowing down and pulling back from hectic routine will herald a new life style and the challenges that crossroad brings. You may shift your focus from work to assisting family and friends or to yourself (imagine that!).

You can start downsizing plans years before the actual retirement by shifting energies to partial employment, by volunteering, or by returning to former hobbies, talents, and interests.

A lifetime of maintaining homes for a family may become maintaining a home for the self and simply one other person. There will not be a need for the 16-piece dish set, two living rooms, or multiple bathrooms. The downsize may include a residential relocation as well as a disbursement of belongings, so time will be dedicated to finding a new nest and there will likely be an adjustment in income.

Questionnaire 4
## RETIREES QUESTIONS TO ASK YOURSELF

Date:

Is this a permanent retirement?

Was this retirement anticipated?

Was this retirement forced through accident or illness?

Are you happy, sad, frightened, excited?

Do you have hobbies or outside interests?

Will you seek part-time work?

Are you financially able to retire?

Will you need to move?

Is downsizing a viable option?

Do you have a plan?

What is it?

Will you volunteer?

Will you travel?

Are you receptive to joining a support group?

Other:

## 2.3 Downsizing for elders / seniors

As with every age group in migration mode, there will be a motivating factor which calls for a reassessment of living arrangements. Some of these moves will be welcomed and embraced with a sense of joy and excitement, a feeling of liberty, as opposed to a loss; a relief from the burden and expense of managing one's belongings and housing of the belongings of others, but to some, the prospect of downsizing will be such an overwhelming thought that it will continue to be delayed, put off, until one day, a triggering event will cause a typically forced and rushed downsize. This happens often in the case of a medical emergency, and at that point, all the thinking of what needs to be done becomes "it must now be done" at a certain time, and place by individuals who may not know your wishes, which is not the most desirable scenario.

Not unlike the steps taken in planning your estate and insurance needs at a younger age, individuals and families should have downsizing plans. This provides for a more responsible taking charge of one's life (at a less expensive cost too). The earlier one makes plans for downsizing scenarios, the more sensible and meaningful the process will be, and the less emotionally challenging and stressful, as situations will have been thought out in advance.

I did not realize that I enjoyed the elderly, having lost my own family at an early age. I did not think of people as young or old actually. They were and are just people, characters, some with quirks and many valuable wisdoms to share. My grandparents were immigrants like so many others of their generation who came to Canada following the war. They were quiet people with spotless homes and good cooking. Adult discussions took place where children were not present. I listened and did as I was told. They were fun to be around as I was the focus of their attention on my rare visits to them. My grandparents lived independently to their last days. Even when they moved into a level floor unit in an apartment (I now realize in retrospect to be one of the first built complexes for older folk), they maintained the furnishings that I was familiar with, but it was more sparse, minimal. The coffee brewing still smelled the same. Grandmother made apple pie and great fish stews. They took me shopping for "better clothing," when I visited wearing the signature Joe Cocker sweater all the rage at the time, and tried to match me with a suitable Finnish boy, which was not a success; the timing was not good. The television channels they watched on an older television were consistent, as was grandmother's apron while she prepared Korput toasts for dipping into coffee. Today, Starbucks has a similar product, called biscotti.

My grandparents moved slowly, but were not feeble, and they still argued delightfully and hugged a lot. They attended social events and danced. Grandmother's ankles would swell and she would roll her nylons down to her ankles and wear grandfather's slippers for warmth, and she would raise her feet onto a chair, arms folded across her ample bosom while watching television or listening to the radio. Grandfather kept his daily ritual of drinking a shot of whiskey and eating a raw onion for breakfast. He was the picture of good health. There were no prescription medications that I ever saw. Hospitals were rarely, if ever attended. Grandfather was tall and handsome with a smiling face, and grandmother was round and huggable with a beautiful face that glowed when Grandfather teased her about her weight, and she flirted back. They were happy together. I never thought in my teen years to ask much of history, but did listen to their stories, so I do have that and the occasional photo, sometimes with people's names written on the back of black and white fluted photos.

I loved grandmother's recipes for beauty. She used black coffee to darken her hair, dipping a rat-tailed comb into the coffee grind liquid daily and combing it through her hair; and she used evaporated beer to make pin curls for that bobbed look.

Fast forward to today. I am now becoming an elder myself. I wish I had more of my grandparent's history in their own words and from their point of view. I have a few items that came my way: a linen tablecloth, carefully preserved, crafted with cutout shapes, hand-stitched; dad's pen and ink set and his athletic medals; love letters between my mother and father, a coupling which was not encouraged by either family; a cookbook; but nothing of my shy grandfather. Whatever happened to their things remains a mystery to me, so I piece together who I am from what memories, photos, and few things I did get from well-meaning friends and neighbours who passed them along to me when I was a young adult. Insurance and wills were not the norm for many of their generation and class.

It is said that children, in looks and mannerisms, skip a generation. I certainly look and act more like my grandparents and my thoughts of them are full of love and warmth.

It may have been comforting to have been around them more, and have some of the things that they valued around me as a reminder of who I am and where I come from. But these are thoughts I take out when sentiment takes up residence in my heart and mind. If only I had thought to ask more, to listen more. If only they knew that their only grandchild thought so highly of them and the lessons they imparted to her. If only they had preserved and imparted their history, told their story for the generations after their own sons and daughters who, until finally the stories of their lives and how they came to be are lost.

Grandfather passed suddenly in his late 80s, and grandmother lived a few years longer, still on her own. However, as her mind began to slip, she became increasingly suspicious of those around her and often bonded with opportunistic individuals she would have best avoided, and I did not possess the experience or maturity to see or act on this, ultimately, to her detriment. She lived peacefully and independently for the most part and died in hospice care after a short illness. She had lost much of her recollections and had reverted to speaking the language she grew up speaking.

To grandparents who may have experienced a separation, conflict or division with your children, your story should be preserved for future generations. As history tends to repeat itself, they may ultimately have conflict with their own children and your grand counsel, history, and wisdoms will be needed or sought by offspring with whom you may have had estrangement.

Children can be innocent bystanders when families experience separation. Children are smart and savvy. They are growing up in difficult times. Perhaps not the kind of times you knew, but other, greater pressures today are no less daunting. Your counsel is not a case of "do as I say," but rather, a case of this is how I dealt successfully with a situation, and this is a situation that had dire consequences. They will draw from that, put it into context in their own lives, hopefully acknowledge experiences shared and move forward in life equipped with at least some sense of how another in their gene pool handled times and situations. Many elders go about their lives not sharing the challenges, horrors, and scarring from the Depression era because they have forgotten or it is too painful to recall and recant, as are thoughts, opinions, and lives wonderfully rebuilt following wars and other catastrophes. Youth should be given the opportunity to see, hear, feel and make sense of things, and this could take a long time. Patient preservation and communication of personal histories and belongings are needed more today than ever.

If you are older, you may be considering moving closer to family such as adult children, grandchildren, brothers or sisters, and so on. You may be considering moving back to childhood towns, cities, or countries. Even though it is to be a happy move, there is still a sense of loss to be experienced. There is leaving of the homes where many memories were made and the added stress of meeting new people, discovering new services, hairdressers, community center activities, and so on.

Choose a new home with the helpful advice of family, friends and other advisors, and think about how to:

- Weigh the positives against the negatives in choosing a new premises, and make a list.

- Get input from friends or family regarding the sale of a family home and relocation to a subsequent new home.

- Ask for their input or ideas on the disposition of belongings.

- Share decorative ideas, furniture, etc.

- Allow family to say goodbye to the family home; possibly offer each a chance to choose an heirloom or sentimental item with history and value.

- Compile a list of possible helpers; define your needs and budget. Check in the Yellow Pages, ask friends, ask community and senior resource centers to point you in the direction of whom to contact and how.

- Allow family a chance to say hello to the new home.

- Suggest they take photos of the old home, and take plants or cuttings from plants they like.

- Walk around the neighborhood together with friends and family, and invite them to walk around the new area.

- Get their input on decorating the new place.

- Go to a community center together.

- Try to arrange a family move-in celebration.

- Plan monthly dinners or regular get-togethers.

## Questionnaire 5
## DOWNSIZING FOR ELDERS AND SENIORS

Date:

What do I need to do?

Do I want to do it all?

Is there an individual or company that can assist in whole or in part?

Will the sale of belongings offset the cost of hiring help?

Other:

Physical limitations and stress can leave you feeling daunted and drained, and you may not have the time or ability to do the inventory, packing and moving. Often the thought of it all can overwhelm an individual to the point of inactivity. Working with other people can nudge from you that place of procrastination even if they are not as good as you, they are around you. There is a need for conversation and motivation to get on with the task, perhaps to the point where you carry on downsizing on your own for a time. If you have done some homework prior to this about companies and individuals to assist, you will be prepared to pick up the phone and start scheduling times to undertake projects.

You may also have a parent or other relative who is suddenly being put into a care facility, coming to a place where independence poses a greater challenge than circumstances permit.

Luckily you are making this decision in a time when downsizing businesses and people for hire are burgeoning and help is available whether moving across the country or around the world into a home or into a retirement community or caregiving facility.

There are individuals and companies available, trained, experienced and insured that are readily available to complete the task for a fee. They can assist in the inventory taking, transporting to the new premises or disposing of the furniture and fixtures utilizing all available marketing. Then they will clean up, leaving the premise, sale or lease ready. If you research, you may find companies that are trained to handle geriatric clients. (See section on choosing a service provider.)

## 2.3a Retirement communities

A retirement community is a housing complex designed for older adults who are generally able to care for themselves; however, assistance from home care agencies is allowed in some communities, and activities and socialization opportunities are often provided. There is no single definition of a retirement community, but some of the characteristics typically are the community must be age-restricted or age-qualified, residents must be partially or fully retired, and the community offers shared services or amenities.

Additionally, there are different types of retirement communities from which older adults can choose:

- Independent living communities, which offer no personal care services.

- Congregate housing, which includes at least one shared meal per day with other residents.

- Mobile homes or RV's for active adults.

- Subsidized housing for lower income older adults.

- Leisure or lifestyle oriented communities or LORCs, which include various amenities.

- Continuing Care Retirement Communities, which are further defined below.

New types of retirement communities are being developed as the population ages including elder co-housing and are fee for service. Some are owned and some are for rent.

Choose a new home with the help of family, friends and other advisors:

- Weigh the positives against the negatives in choosing a new premises, make a list.

- Get input from friends or family regarding the sale of family home and relocation to subsequent new home.

- Ask for their input or ideas on the disposition of belongings.

- Share decorative ideas, furniture, etc.

- Consider new color or style.

- Allow family to say goodbye to the family home, possibly offer each a chance to choose an heirloom or sentimental item with history and value.

- Allow family a chance to say hello to the new home.
- Suggest they take photos of the old home, take plants or cuttings.
- Walk around the neighborhood together reminding them that they can return, invite them to walk around the new area.
- Get their input into decorating the new place.
- Go to a community center together.
- Try to engage a family move in celebration.
- Plan monthly dinners or regular get togethers.

## 2.3b  Nursing homes

Definition: a private institution providing residential accommodations with health care, especially for elderly people.

The relevance to downsizing to a retirement community or nursing home is the square footage of the facility or residence that individual(s) will have for their belongings they wish to take with them, or for which they will possibly purchase. There are all types and sizes of retirement homes in retirements communities, from luxurious fully serviced homes to simple, easy to care for units in complexes. In the case of nursing homes, space can be very limited, medically oriented, from shared to even one room. Therefore, researching the future facility will help you decide what stays and what goes. You may decide to purchase furniture that acts also as clever storage units as in the case of ottomans, making maximum use of limited space.

Choosing your future home will depend on your needs. Will you need permanent accommodation or temporary accommodation?
Try to obtain referrals from others who have faced similar situations, visit the establishments, get a feel for how people seem to be, happy, sad, and so on. Do the premises look clean and well cared for? Check with your physician or other advisors as to what you may best be suited. Ensure that you consider distance from friends and relatives for visiting times and contact.

Individuals will have to be approved to enter a nursing facility, recommended by a medical practitioner and other health professionals such as

They then go on a waiting list to enter a facility as space becomes available, or if they have adequate income, they will enter one of their choice.

Some things to consider in choosing a nursing facility selection are:

- Location.
- Atmosphere.
- Menus.
- Activities.
- Personal services.
- Attitude of staff.
- Green space.
- Demeanor of residents.

Visit the facility at different times to get an overall view.

### A Letter from Someone Who Has Downsized

First with my wife's mother, who was in failing healthy, we had to select a home but were re-stricted by having to take the first opening we could get. She ended up in a nice enough place near a lake, but was far from where her husband was living. We went on a wait list for new housing and care facilities that were being built. There were full pay beds and subsidized beds and rooms. We took a subsidized room which was a really nice place and we are happy with her care there. I think it is important to get a place that is close to home so relatives can see their family without having to travel too far and this encourages more visits hopefully. If you have the money or have a government that financially subsidizes care for seniors, you can be picky about where the seniors end up living. You can and should check out the reputation of the facility for food, staff and general overall layout and cleanliness, etc. The size of the place will determine how much of their belongings can accompany them.

A friend got into assisted living first. He was able to go out for breakfasts and buy food at the local grocery store on his scooter. As time went by, he came incontinent so he had to be moved out of assisted living into a complex care wing. He had the funds to pay for a room when it became available, otherwise he would have to take the first room available in his area. The rate for this care was upwards of $6,000.00 per month. Being in touch and taking direction from local health authorities helped a lot and are available to assist caregivers if they know to ask for it. There are services provided, such a medical administration daily for a fee. The help is there if you know where to look and who to ask.

— Donald

## A Letter from Someone Who Has Downsized

I have a close family, they have always helped each other but things went downhill when my father, the family patriarch, took ill and was placed into nursing care and then passed away. It rocked the family even though we were expecting his decline and we were overwhelmed with dealing with grief and mom. I am an atypical sandwich generation person. When I was not with my aging parents and aging parents in law, I am with my grandchildren and children. At one point both parents were in the hospital at the same time. I was hoping to keep them together as a couple in the nursing home but then my father got very sick and they were separated. I lived with the big G, guilt, sibling rivalry wherein three sisters all with strong ideas of how to do things and when, and some of who gets what and why. The parents seemed fine at dinners, so there was not an obvious indicator that they needed more help than what was believed. The challenge was not financial, they had good pensions. Mom was going into an apartment near a nursing home with most of her treasures as this is a comfort to her and reminder of the nice things she had acquired in life. Admittedly going through and preparing her for the move was a childhood heaven as good memories were relived. Many of her furnishings were left in a condo, which she rented out for a while while she was adjusting to her new place. A lot of things were given to family and other organizations. Just because we don't want it, doesn't mean it is not needed. We were able to hire (by sponsoring) a personal caregiver for mom in her home to delay the cost of extended care until such time as she runs out of funds or is needing greater care. With another family member who was resistant to moving, we did it in stages. First was to treat it as a temporary move until a period of time had passed and then moved to sell and dispose of her home and belongings that were not needed. Balancing life, and caregiving for older and younger generations is a challenge and I am not as physically fit as I once was. It is a very difficult time of life.

— Sandra

You may be considering moving closer to family, adult children, grandchildren, brothers or sisters or friends for comfort and safety. You may be pining for your childhood towns, cities, or countries. In many cases you may not be able to make a move back to another country due to restrictions. You will have to check with government authorities for immigrations and visa requirements. You may not be able to make a permanent move, but temporary stays may be possible if you are adequately covered for any unexpected health issues.

Before you make any plans, these ideas should be discussed with all parties. Here are a few questions to think about and ask in your own words and in good time.

Questionnaire 6
## DISCUSSING RETIREMENT HOMES AND DOWNSIZING WITH AN ELDER

Date:

Are you needing to move closer to family/friends? If so, why?

Are you wanting to move closer to family/friends? If so, why?

Have you discussed this with family/friends?

Are they receptive and welcoming?

How did they express their invitation to you?

Will you have a private space if in their home?

What furniture and belongings are you able to accommodate?

What compensation will be required, rent, utilities, etc., of you?

Are you permitted pets or visitors?

Will you have medical needs ?

Do you have access to a medical service provider nearby?

Will you need transportation (to medical appointments, etc)?

Do you have financial resources to afford you independence?

If you will require financial assistance, has this been clearly discussed?

Do you have an outside support network in the event of conflicts?

Have you prepared a budget together?

Are you able to contribute in family or friend dynamics?

Will you be able and welcome to contribute to family meals and outings?

Is there a senior recreation center nearby?

Who will assist in the downsizing and move?

Can you afford to hire a downsizing service provider?

Will you be able to schedule times away for respite?

Are there unresolved family conflicts?

Would this be a mutually beneficial downsize move?

Would a move into assisted living be better for you?

Would a move into assisted living be better for family or friends?

What research have you done?

Other:

Fortunately, you are making a decision in a time when there are caregivers and downsizing businesses trained and qualified to assist. Use the advice of trusted advisors, ensure you have a return plan in the event that the situation does not meet with your expectations, and make good plans based on many sources of advice.

## 2.4 Downsizing for the disabled

A disabled person may be experiencing physical or mental illness or injury that limits or constrains movement, perceptions, and activities. A disability can be apparent or hidden and is not obvious. A disability may have evolved since birth, as a result of a health event, or other personal catastrophe.

The individual may have lived a life disability free prior to the disabling, and has wishes and objectives about how his or her life is to be lived in the event of an incapacitation. There are still favorite books, music, items of art and so on which are treasured by the disabled person. These people may have lived a time independently but can no longer.

A caregiver must be observant and patient. A caregiver should work with the disabled individual utilizing communication tools to help a disabled individual relay wishes, maintain comfort and familiarity. Caregivers may be able to assist in part with things such as inventory taking and decision making in sorting and disposing of goods.

Tools and equipment may be modified to assist the functioning of the disabled individual. Easy-to-hold pens, markers, and tape dispensers may be acquired. Consider a tape recorder for instructing and consider videotaping for reference the responses of an individual as he or she is questioned on needs and wants.

As plans and checklists are important in all downsizing projects, they are all the more so in dealing with the estate of a disabled person. Be sensitive and aware of the individual's ability to communicate. Work around limitations allowing for additional time and care in communications.

The disabled may have additional challenges in their downsizing tasks. Sometimes the disability is apparent and visible, and often the disability, such as multiple sclerosis or arthritis may not be apparent. People may have:

- Limited energy due to chronic illness or pain.
- Mobility restrictions.
- Financial restrictions.
- Frustration due to limitations of movement.
- Pride or embarrassment that may preclude requests for help.
- Isolation that precludes who to ask for help.
- Unawareness of how much help is needed.
- Extended time needed to accomplish tasks.
- Limited network of support.

There are sources of help for disabled downsizers.

- Physicians may provide assistance or outreach recommendations.
- Community support workers may provide assistance or recommendations.

- If pensioned, human resources divisions of the employer may provide assistance or recommendations.

- Family members or friends may make recommendations.

For example, a physician may not know of a resource to assist directly, but an office manager in the physician's office may provide information or literature as to where a helpful resource may be located.

Consider:

- Moving projects along at a slower pace.

- Using larger print checklist if sight is challenged, or read it and write down answers.

- Observing scheduled rest periods.

- Requesting assistance from friends, relatives, neighbors.

- Practicing patience.

- Confirming the objective with feedback (use photos) if necessary for pointing.

- Additional prepping (e.g.) moving items to comfortable level for labeling packaging.

- Not obstructing paths, halls with boxes etc.

- Confirming approval, directions and consent with feedback from questions.

- Providing useful suggestions.

For the disabled invididual, prepare a video using your cell phone or digital camera. Break it into small sections, room by room if necessary. Describe what you need to have done or ask if there is someone with patience who would help you prepare the video(s). Students may be an ideal, affordable resource to complete this task. If you prepare the checklists yourself, try to have two copies of all you prepare either in writing or by video so that you have a copy and the caregiver or service provider has a copy. This way you have a reminder and a reference of what you have done and prepared.

If finances are a further challenge as they can be to a disabled person, consider trading a service for an item. Make certain, though, to have an agreement in writing if possible as to what the trade is for. For example you may trade a vintage record or book for every hour of work.

Use Questionnaire 7: Downsizing for the Disabled to think through issues specific to downsizing for those with special challenges.

Questionnaire 7
## DOWNSIZING FOR THE DISABLED

Date:

What are your needs or the needs of the disability (permanent or temporary)?

Would assistance be required and how can assistance be given?

Is there a next of kin or close friend nearby?

Is there a budget for obtaining assistance and if so does it cover smaller costs or larger expenses such as a moving crew?

What makes your (or their) environment a happy place for them e.g. fresh air, music, cooking scents?

Are they working with a community or social service provider or possibly an insurer to provide funds or help?

How do they pay for things? Cash, check, credit, or debit?

Can pleasurable away times be planned (if there is lots going on in the house) or as a reward for accomplishments?

How do they get their meals and is there adequate food or provisions during the quite possibly busy project?

Are there favorite plans that need attending to and if so can instructions be communicated?

If there is a scheduled tea or coffee time or schedule for physiotherapy or prescription medication, nap time?

Is there a favorite pastime or hobby e.g., listening to a favorite classical musical station?

What are the physical or mental constraints that would hinder a downsizing task?

Other:

## 2.5 Downsizing and wildlife considerations

Wildlife matters. Wildlife in your life matters, too, and they need consideration for the loss of you and care you may have provided either with safe shelter, an unobstructed pathway, natural foods provided, water during dry spells, or food during cold spells. Consider birds, feral animals, neighbors' pets, deer, raccoons, and other animals.

When planning a downsize wherein you relocate, provide written summary to inform other caring people of the known or observed habits of wildlife in your area. Make a list of wildlife and their visiting habits.

- Notify animal control in your jurisdiction or neighbors to feed them when you can.
- Notify animal assistance groups.
- Notify neighbors and parks people.

Think about communicating acivities about:

- Deer sleeping in the yard and grazing on grasses
- Raccoons taking shelter in higher trees
- Hummingbirds feeding twice daily
- Fresh water left out in hot months and colder temperatures
- Birdseed scattered over winter months
- No pesticides used on fruit trees or near gardens the bees enjoy.

## 2.6 Downsizing with pets

As our loyal friends, we need to consider the physical and mental well-being of our pets. Animals are intuitive and sensitive to stress. A downsize will bewilder pets and so we must take precautions to ensure they do not endure more stress.

The first way we can downsize with pets is to have them properly neutered or spayed, to prevent having to downsize pets themselves.

As a society of pet lovers, we acquire and carefully tend to our pets' needs. The good care results in some long lived pets in our lives. There are times when we can no longer care for our pets, as in the case of downsize due to a medical situation, or when we have to move homes and animals are no longer allowed to stay with us. As traumatizing as this is for the people, it is all the more so for the animals, birds, and others in our care.

Communicate for your pets. Make sure they maintain their regular diet, place to sleep or favorite blanket, and maintain their exercise regime.

Prepare a list to accompany the pet. Make a list and describe the pet's life in your care:

- Eating and drinking habits.

- Exercise habits.

- Favorite rituals

- Where the animal normally sleeps.

- If the pet has been living with other pets (they may suffer depression from separation).

- If the pet as lived quietly, with older people, younger people, etc.

- The breed, and gender of the pet.

- Age of the pet.

- Dental history.

- Veterinarian.

- Things that frighten the pet.

- Things that make the pet happy.

- Words that the pet responds to.

- What kind of weather the pet most prefers.

- What kind of sounds the pet was used to hearing.

- How often the pet has its nails groomed.

- If it responds to one gender over another.

- If it has a best friend that can still be called to go on walks.

- Other behavior to help a new owner make the pet's transition as comfortable as possible.

## 2.7 Downsizing for the deceased or bereaved

Once you have legal permission and assurance that you are permitted to deal with an estate of a deceased person, such as confirming that you are an executor or administrator of an estate, start with making a to-do list to help orient yourself to the impending task. Progress slowly if you are assisting a spouse, family member, or friend of the deceased. Sort and organize by subject and review the belongings with the spouse, family member, or friend of the deceased. Pack and remove belongings in stages, and direct or take direction as to how to dispose of, or sell the items.

If you are dealing with an emotionally charged situation that will require more time for decision making, consider moving belongings out of sight, into storage containers or units. Dispose of personal items such as underwear, socks, and hats.

For items that are difficult to decide what to do with, keep them stored for now until a decision can be made.

Keep personal papers, banking documents, identification, taxes, etc., in a separate accessible weatherproof container, and wait for directions from tax planner, or lawyer in matters of settling the estate and dealing with government requests such a filing for pensions, registering the death, and obtaining probate.

Bereaved individuals may need to delay to a less emotional time to avoid the possibility of making hasty decisions.

Be aware when selling items for an estate that you attain fair market value to avoid possible problems with heirs of an estate, and that you should never sell items that belong to someone else without permission (e.g., you have been named executor).

Downsizing in a bereavement situation is compounded grief. The death of a loved one is one of life's most difficult challenges for the survivor and in addition to dealing with a loss and the range of emotions accompanying that will be the added stress of having to contend with the departed one's belongings. If at all possible, try not to deal with this alone. If you feel this is a project you want to contend with on your own, you are advised to join a support group or keep in communication with someone you trust daily, weekly, and monthly to share the ups and downs.

Caregivers are encouraged to take the initiative in reaching out to the bereaved. Attend a grief counseling support group or take a grief counseling course to help you deal effectively with others. Understanding grief also assists your own life's challenges, so it will not be time wasted.

Grief is not predictable nor is there a set time period in which people complete the grieving process. Those working with the bereaved, and those who have suffered a loss may benefit by reading about the theory of the five stages of grief, known as the Kübler-Ross model.

Some people experience shock for longer than others and decision-making during this time can be very unpredictable. Caregivers must listen with compassion, sometimes in silence, allowing the person to speak. Be supportive even if the individual is reacting adversely. It could be emotions speaking. Ask, don't tell, in a sensitive way.

Suggestions for helping when stepping up to provide assistance to someone in grief:

- Communicate. Call, visit, send a note, attend in person, bring food, or flowers.
- Ask questions, be present and observe.
- Do not ask closed-ended questions that command one word replies, such as "Are you okay?" or "I hope you are okay," but rather, "What did you do today?" to encourage dialogue.
- Offer tangible help.
- Be patient and empathetic, do not judge emotional outbursts or actions in the grief period. Listen attentively.
- Validate their grief and don't forget the healing powers of a hug
- Check that the person is eating properly and sleeping and functioning safely.
- Encourage them to see their health service provider and try to accompany them.
- Encourage activity (even if refused) Try to get them outside in fresh air and sunlight or with other people. Ask them to keep you company on a walk, Offer to take them to grief counseling.

- If you do favors, keep a diary or notes or photos of what you have done for them as they may not remember and need to see for themselves later, as in the case of clearing out clothing of the deceased.

- If you realize a downsize is pending, start to gather information, brochures, literature for them and be prepared to start giving them ideas with decision making

- Research some downsizing service providers to assist when the time is ready

- Be patient and let them come to you as they are ready, willing and able. You will find an individual in shock, denial, suffering, anger, anxiety, fatigue.

- Take care of yourself so that in taking care of others, you do not become ill yourself. Try to stay strong and positive.

- If you need a reprieve, ask another person to help you provide support to the grieving person.

- Consider going to a support group for grief counseling and caregivers if you have not done so.

## 2.8 Downsizing due to bankruptcy, insolvency, or financial catastrophe

Individuals who face a relocation or a downsizing due to a financial catastrophe such as a bankruptcy should be aware that there are laws, rules, and regulations with respect to the disposition of personal belongings such as furniture, goods, and vehicles.

For example, if items have been purchased on credit or pledged to secure a loan, the lender may be a secured creditor who has first rights to the items. Before disposing of furniture, vehicles, goods and so on in many jurisdictions, the secured creditor has the right, with proper documentation, to enforce seizing and liquidating to offset or pay off the debt.

In a Canadian bankruptcy, for example, an individual's estate is governed by federal and provincial laws dictating the disposal of assets, so generally two authorities may be required before assets can be disposed of. A bankruptcy professional will provide the guidelines on this.

Before you consider selling or disposing of any belongings:

1. Take a physical inventory or visually document the inventory.

2. You will need to ensure that the belongings are not pledged as security for a debt, or being held as collateral by contractual agreement or loan. This may require a check in a government held registry as to ownership restrictions.

3. Check with a bankruptcy professional as to what items of value can be retained by the debtor, or the debtor's estate. For example, in Canada there are provincial exemptions which state what value of property and what property can be retained by a debtor.

In Canada, check with a trustee or the Office of the Superintendent of Bankruptcy for a guideline. In the United States check with a trustee or the bankruptcy court. In Great Britain and Australia, check with a trustee.

If the financial setback is the catalyst to moving to a smaller space, there will undoubtedly be a great deal of emotion and possibly a rushed timeline.

Consider storing your belongings with friends, family, or at a commercial site for a period of reorganizing time, or grieving time and decide to deal with it in the months following settling into a smaller space, thus allowing yourself time to adjust before conducting a fire sale type of asset disposal.

You may not be permitted to dispose of your belongings until clearance is received from your bankruptcy professional.

---

Helpful Hint

Take digital pictures of your things, save them to a USB key or on a CD or DVD or post them privately online in one of the many photo storage places so you can view them without having to physically go to them.

This is particularly helpful if your computer or other equipment is subject to seizure in the bankruptcy.

---

Once you have permission from the authorized representative of the bankruptcy, you may use the photos to post advertisements to sell the goods if that is your intention. If you or someone you know is intending to go bankrupt, or has taken the steps to get bankruptcy protection, chances are there will be a downsize or departure from an owned or rental home as well.

Belongings in the home may be securing a loan. Permission from a bankruptcy professional is required and security documents need to be validated before keeping, selling, or disposing of belongings.

If a security document is not valid, e.g., errors are found, the bankruptcy professional may take an interest on behalf of the estate, and require the belongings to be valued and sold.

If the belongings are free and clear and the trustee has no interest in them on behalf of the estate, the individual may be allowed keep them and do with them what they want. This is an issue which is dealt with in the beginning of the process, and questions can be asked during an initial meeting (often at no charge) with a bankruptcy professional.

## 2.9 Downsizing by caregivers

Downsizing for family, a friend, acquaintance, or neighbor? If you know someone who will be downsizing or simply moving, you may wish to offer help. In the case of an elderly or disabled person you may have been asked to provide assistance in preparing an individual for a relocation.

What is your relationship with the individual? What is your motivation for providing assistance?

Are there clear instructions communicated ? Will there be financial consideration for services provided or items given in exchange for time?

Are you a caregiver with formal training or a knowledgeable understanding of what is needed by an individual in a downsizing situation? Can you perform some or all of the required duties?

Can you help engage a downsizing service provider to perform some or all of the duties?

A large component of downsizing is the disposal of belongings, either by selling, gifting, trashing, recycling, or donating. Although people are free to do what they want with their belongings within lawful boundaries, there are some things to consider in so doing, for example the purchasing or acquiring of belongings from a family member may give the appearance of a conflict of interest or having an advantage over others who may be interested in the item or belonging and ethical interests or value received may be challenged. If there is a possibility of a conflict of interest, or in a situation where your actions or motivation may be challenged, it is best to seek legal opinion.

Before volunteering time to assist another, consider whether:

- You will expect, accept, or decline compensations for time spent.

- You will expect, accept, or decline reimbursement for expenses.

- You will clearly explain your physical and time constraints to the individual(s) . (While it may be admirable to offer help, if you are unable to complete the work expected of you, or if you become disinterested or discouraged, you may be hindering instead of helping. Disclose your limitations from the onset so the individual(s) can make alternative arrangements, a Plan B.

- You will possibly have a conflict of interest with family members or others.

- You are legally permitted to (sell) deal with the belongings and are they free and clear of encumbrance(s).

- You understand the concept of duty of care? (The requirement that a person act toward others and the public with watchfulness, attention, caution. and prudence that a reasonable person in the circumstances would. If a person's actions do not meet this standard, the acts could be considered negligent and any damages resulting may be claimed in a lawsuit).

## Questionnaire 8
## QUESTIONS TO ASK BEFORE DOWNSIZING FOR ANOTHER

Date:

Do you have legal authority to deal with this situation? Is there a lawyer, accountant, or financial advisor who knows the affairs of the individual? Is there a trustee or executor (or executrix) appointed who will act or provide direction?

Are you aware of any family or asset conflicts? If so seek legal advice on the best way to proceed, before proceeding if possible.

Will you need the assistance of a public trustee or public guardian in order to act on assets in peril (or weather, pests, rodents and so on) until legal authority is established?

Once you have established authority to act and this has to be a priority, you can proceed. It is recommended that you contact a lawyer or solicitor immediately and take instruction or direction from him or her or take as to how to best proceed. The family lawyer would be a bonus if there is one.

Do not ignore or abandon the living individuals who may have fallen ill. Visit and provide support. Ask questions, if possible, as to their next of kin, and legal representatives. If the individual is unable to communicate, there may be a "living will" direction with the hospital or physician and a lawyer's name associated with whom you may refer to for further guidance.

You may need accommodation in the case of an out of town situation or for convenience. If it is approved by the solicitor, executor (or executrix) or guardian, you should phone and ask first and the premises is secure and a health environment for you, you can use that as your base to visit the individual, make funeral arrangements if needed and to commence to-do lists inventory taking and dealing with packing.

If you are not the executor or do not hold a power of attorney, and you are speaking with a lawyer or legal representative, they must be advised of the circumstances as to:

a.  Why you were notified to assist.

b.  Who notified you?

c.  What the urgency is (an eviction of infirm tenant) or assets in peril or jeopardy of damage) including the time constraint.

d.  What your relationship to the individual is.

e.  What permissions you have and in what form?

f.  Request what permissions you need and from whom.

Be aware that there will be costs involved. Ask legal representatives for an idea of the costs at the onset, who will be responsible for paying them and if there is any reimbursement.

Keep a list of all expenses together with receipts. This includes travel, telephone costs and so on. When obtaining quotes for service providers such as a downsizing company, try to obtain more than one quote, three being a good number to compare value for services.

Do the same for storage facilities In the event of probate scenarios or to allow time to take an inventory if an immediate vacancy needs to be effected. Allow time to digest and conduct the downsizing effectively.

If you have the authorized permission, you can call a downsize company, obtain their contract details and also their payment requirements to help you make the decision. Meet with representatives and provide the authority for them to proceed.

It is recommended that you take photos of the premises to use in subsequent decision making, particularly if items have been put into storage pending legalities as the individual may recover and return to independent living. This will help the individual understand what you have done, or will help a trustee, executor or guardian understand what actions you took and what is in storage or an auction company to provide a value estimate on goods.

Other:

# 3

## Goal Setting and Planning

Goal setting works! Goal setting keeps you motivated and moving forward, and helps in decision making.

You can make a diagram if you are visually motivated, or you write it down or use a program designed for charting goals — whatever works best for you.

## 1. Reasons to Set a Goal

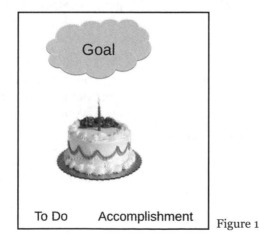

Figure 1

As Figure 1 shows, there is more to baking than just baking a cake.

Something as simple as baking a cake can mean taking dozens of steps from assembling the ingredients to the end result of delivering the cake. A successful cake baked takes planning, but we don't think of it as such. Is your goal something you want or something you need?

For caregivers, the goal may be as simple as following the instructions of the person downsizing, or helping him or her to find the assistance needed. It should be reviewed and measured against or along with your scheduling availability, your resource availability, budget, and it should follow legal and regulatory direction.

Use the "Who, What, Why, Where, When, How" formula to make plans to achieve the goal.

This may seem wordy, or not important, but it is surprising how many people do not make a goal and plans when they tackle large projects which will result in more wasted time and energy than if they had been made.

The first item on a downsize to-do list is to set a goal, following by plans to support the goal.

Consider goal-setting and planning as planning a road trip. Decide where you will be going, how long it will take, what stops to make along the way, and what troubleshooting may be anticipated, as well as backup plans if things do not go as planned.

Revisit and reset as you progress, for example weekly, monthly, semi-annually, and annually.

No matter whether you are downsizing for yourself or you are assisting another as a caregiver, a goal must be set and accompanied by plans to achieve the goal. Not having a goal is akin to getting in your car to go on a road trip without knowing your destination and what you need to get you there.

Goal-setting keeps you motivated and moving forward, and helps in decision making. A goal must be written down to be most effective, and goals can change as needed, but setting a goal defines what it is you are doing, and is a reminder to you and others of your motivation.

Display your goal boldly where you can see it daily.

A goal can start as a lofty ideal such as "I wish I could" and progress to a written "I must do" or "I want this to happen." The wheels are then set in motion and this sets the stage for action.

A goal must be specific in nature, measurable, realistic, achievable, and written down.

Goals are not just for businesses; goals are set by individuals every day, we may just not recognize them as goals. An everyday goal:

- Provides a vision of the end result.

- Motivates you forward.

- Is particularly desirable for large or challenging tasks.

## 2. Mission Statement

The goal in the case of the following mission statement is to downsize and move to a smaller place:

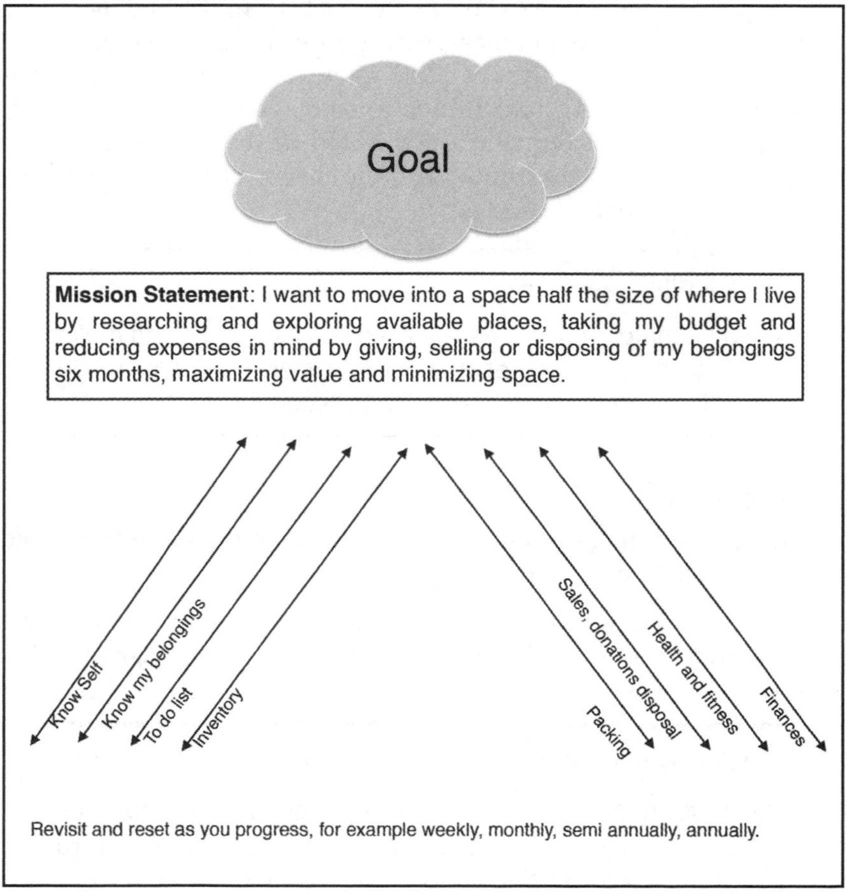

**Goal**

**Mission Statement:** I want to move into a space half the size of where I live by researching and exploring available places, taking my budget and reducing expenses in mind by giving, selling or disposing of my belongings six months, maximizing value and minimizing space.

Know Self
Know my belongings
To do list
Inventory

Sales, donations disposal
Health and fitness
Finances
Packing

Revisit and reset as you progress, for example weekly, monthly, semi annually, annually.

Figure 2

## 2.1 Writing your mission statement

Now that you have written down the goal, you need an action (mission) statement, or what is known as an affirmation statement to reinforce and communicate your determination to achieve your goal. This is not unlike posting a reminder on a fridge when one goes on a diet or has another objective one wants to achieve.

"I will move to a new, smaller residence that meets my needs physically, emotionally, and financially, so that I can live safely, conveniently, and independently. I wish to continue to enjoy volunteering (walking, biking, boating) and connected to the community. I will do this in six months and will offset the cost of the move with the selling my belongings."

Or, a caregiver might write: "I will assist the individual move to a new smaller residence that meets their needs physically, emotionally, and financially, so that they can live safely, conveniently, and independently as they wish to continue to enjoy volunteering (walking, biking, boating) and remaining connected to the community. This must be done within six months and the costs will be offset with the selling of belongings."

---

Helpful Hint

As you update, add or cross off accomplished tasks and make newer to-do lists, do not throw away older, previously made lists. File them by date to review your progress.

---

## 3. Planning

You have a written goal and an affirmation statement; now you need to make plans to meet your goal.

Plans are simply to-do lists on steroids. Plans provide the necessary details and steps for getting something accomplished in the future.

---

The goal is to move to a smaller premises.

The mission statement is "I (who) will downsize my premises (what) affording me the opportunity to move to a smaller place that is more manageable and less expensive to maintain (why) closer to the downtown area (where)within one year's time (when) by donating and selling half of my belongings (how)."

---

Plans provide details of how the goal will be achieved. By answering the following questions. They can be simple or they can be elaborate. By following the who, what, why, where, when and how format and leaving nothing out, you will have commenced a roadmap to achieving what you want. This is applicable to any plan you make. Try it, it works!

Here are a few examples you could alter to your situation:

A Plan by an Individual

| Who | You |
|---|---|
| What | Downsize Home Belongings |
| Why | Retirement |
| Where | At Home |
| When | January to June this year |
| How | Sell house, sell belongings, move by doing the following things: (list everything) |

Mission (Action) Statement: to inventory, pack store or dispose of household belongings, preserving care of the belongings, moving the belongings or selling the belongings maximizing value, in a 30-day period.

A Plan by a Caregiver

| Who | Company A, a downsize company |
|---|---|
| What | carry out the tasks of moving an individual |
| Why | Contractual Agreement |
| Where | City of Anywhere |
| When | June of this year |
| How | Inventory, pack, move and relocate individual (list all tasks in contract) |

Mission (Action) Statement: to inventory, pack store or dispose of household belongings, preserving care of the belongings, moving the belongings or selling the belongings maximizing value, in a 30-day period.

The client/friend needs to move due to health concerns.

That is it. It starts simple.

Whenever you hit a snag in your task, refer to the plan you made (and will continually revise); break it down into smaller parts to see what needs to be done or improved to get back on track in the area that is causing a challenge.

## 4. Setting and Establishing Priorities

Prioritizing is establishing the importance of attending to tasks in the order of urgency or importance.

People make families their top priorities. It is one of the driving reasons behind estate planning and obtaining life insurance. Downsizing is a life succession plan. A good downsizing plan with clearly defined priorities will make it easier on caregivers to assist and easier for an individual to meet the goal that has been set.

A good downsize plan is the exit strategy that takes into consideration any number of many what if? scenarios:

- What if the children move out?
- What if I get ill?
- What if my partner passes away?
- What if I wish to move nearer to my family?
- What if I can no longer maintain my home?
- What if I can no longer afford my home?
- What if I wish to travel and an opportunity comes up?
- What if the children move back home?
- Do I sell or store my things?

For example, no one wants to talk about death and life insurance and yet the financial catastrophe resulting in not dealing with it in one's youth or healthy years is devastating in the absence of coverage. People who have foregone paying a few extra dollars a month in planning for security will admit regretting not having attended to it when they could have and should have.

Downsizing plans rank up there with choosing life insurance and investing and estate planning and it doesn't cost anything to make plans and at the very least to ease the burden of stress on oneself and one's helpful caregivers when, not if, the time comes.

You will become focused when you:

- Start thinking about the subject of downsizing for yourself and as a caregiver.

- Scan magazines and other periodicals for this subject on a regular basis.

- Make to-do lists.

- Revisit and revise plans daily, weekly, monthly as needed.

- Take steps toward your goal (an hour a day and upwards).

- Reward yourself for accomplishments along the way.

- Visit or volunteer at a nursing home.

- Visit consignment and second-hand stores to see how belongings are to others.

- Attend craft fairs to see the creative ways things are recycled.

- Attend caregiving seminars to be prepared when called upon.

- Visit furniture stores to see the latest trends in furnishings.

- Review to your to-do lists daily.

What does your life to-do list look like today? Think about the downsizing situation you are facing. Read up on it. Make it a familiar topic daily. Who are the people involved or who will be impacted? What time limits are you working with? Are there budgeting restrictions?

# 5. Scheduling

Now that you have set a goal together with an inspiring statement and you have made plans,you are ready to get on with your downsizing task. To meet the deadlines you have set you need to schedule tasks by priority.

The first thing you need is a calendar. You may opt for one with dates that are displayed with boxes that you can write in, or you can choose a year-at-a-glance one. You may also use one of many scheduling apps for your hand held device which have the added benefit of alarms and reminder features.

Why is scheduling important?

- Keeps you organized and realistic.

- Tasks broken down into manageable activities.

- Keeps you on target and improves performance.

- Visual pattern of activity helps you stay balanced.
- Ensures your project doesn't interfere with other projects or appointments.
- Helps you analyze your progress and prioritize duties.

Table 4
## SAMPLE INITIAL TO-DO LISTS

| To-Do 1 | To-Do 2 | To-Do 3 |
|---|---|---|
| Sell house. Rent new accommodation. Find a townhouse. Find a retirement home. Find a nursing home. | Interview realtor. Research availabilities. | Choose a realtor / commit to price. Make appointment to view. Make appointment to view. Commit to a lease/ agreement |
| Make a list of advisors | Make appointments to see advisors | Meet with advisors and start making plans. |
| Schedule times to Declutter. Sort. Organize. | Make an inventory of items to distribute and obtain packing containers | Research places to distribute belongings. |
| Sell Donate Dispose | Organize items to: Sell. Donate. Dispose. | Distribute items to: Sell. Donate. Dispose. |
| Other: | Other: | Other: |

This is particularly helpful for procrastinators or busy people. Scheduling keeps you on target and breaks down what you are doing into manageable tasks so that there is no overlap with other projects or appointments. It is a visual reminder and review of what you have accomplished and what you have yet to do.

You will need to initially schedule a review of your goals and plans, and time to do your Know Yourself or Know Your Caregivers questionnaire (in Chapter 4). You will need time to review your support team advisors; take inventory; research, sort, declutter, and assemble supplies and equipment; and attend appointments.

To get motivated, try something you find fun to get you in the mood.

- Put on the music.
- Bake a fruit crumble.
- Dance, as a warm up exercise.

Then:

- Refer to your questionnaires and lists.
- Display your goal as a motivation as well as your affirmation statement or photo.
- Plan nutrition and meals (e.g. slow cooker) to avoid time away from the job.
- Take breaks and stretch.
- Task help for strenuous jobs such as box moving .
- Make room for the transfer of items to e.g. garage, spare room.

Do not forget:

- Reward yourself for a job well done.
- Feel good about yourself and your accomplishments.

Suggested scheduling for a time for taking inventory: Pick a bag with a flat bottom. Call it your project bag (so it can set on the floor or furniture (table or chair) Add to it, your calendar, a pad of paper (for making a to-do list), pens, stickers, a flashlight, a camera (ideally) and other tokens you will use to get started. Include items that inspire you, such as a picture of your desired future premises, a print out of your goals and plans. The bag should be large enough to hold it all, but small enough to be portable. Practical can be attractive too.

Try using motivating cues or rituals to get you in the mood such as putting on music (if that inspires you) a warm up exercise. Turn your phone off, or set for messages. Set an alarm for one hour (you can expand this to more hours later).

Take the bag with you from room to room and add to your to do list or inventory list. The bag will be representative of the downsize project to you, family, friends and others. Add articles and pamphlets about downsizing to your bag. Ask friends and relatives to add to it. A veritable trick or treat bag of downsizing.

As you add to your to-do list, the bag will become fuller and you may have to start emptying your bag, such as moving collected brochures and magazines to a file folder.

When you put the bag away, that signals a shut off time for you. When you take it out again that signals a commence time. Spend time reviewing what you wrote on your to-do list, make changes such as checking off what you have done, and add what further needs to be done.

This puts the task in one place and at the ready. If accepting assistance, you can hand the bag to a helper along with instructions from your to do list.

If you are a caregiver, you can use the project bag to carry on with the downsizing, and to keep track of your progress with the individual or in their absence.

# 6. Inventory Taking

We are familiar with inventory taking as being an activity a business performs to keep track of its things, by regularly counting them, describing and itemizing what has been sold, is missing, or damaged. Recommendations and actions are then made to replace, renew, increase, or decrease quantity. Inventory taking is used in the sale and purchase of businesses to arrive at valuations. With the progress of technology to scanning of coded labeling, the personnel taking of inventory has changed and establishments rarely have to close for inventory anymore as inventory analysis is done mathematically and often off site.

The evolution of inventory taking has been remarkable for business but it is not an evolution that translated beneficially in terms of accuracy and time for individuals in their homes and with their own belongings.

## 6.1 What is inventory taking in a downsize project and why is it important?

We take stock and inventory even though we may not call it that in some of the following scenarios.

We obtain home and other possession insurance by answering questions provided to us by insurers regarding the value and quantity and condition of our insurable belongings. We sign declarations and pay fees to safeguard values in the event of loss or damage.

We obtain mortgages based on home values.

We prepare wills directing distribution of our belongings to beneficiaries.

We prepare descriptions of belongings to offer them for sale.

Probate and taxation may require asset descriptions, and inventories are required for estate sales. If an inventory being performed is for an estate sale, it may be performed at the residence or from a storage facility or auction house. A sale can also be conducted online. Time and money can be saved by preparing for the sale by itemizing belongings in a logical and viewable way.

In the absence of a descriptive inventory, the above may not be possible or difficult to estimate. Keeping receipts for items purchased many years before may not always be realistic. If you have ever suddenly realized that something in your home is missing and are struggling to answer the question "when did you last see the item?" you will realize the importance of knowing your belongings.

Taking periodic inventory is good, but taking an inventory for the purpose of downsizing is necessary to assess importance, assign values, and for aiding in decision making for the elimination and disposition of our things.

Consider how a written and a photo inventory could work well together. A photo is taken and an inventory is written later from viewing the photo at large size.

### Table 5
### WRITTEN INVENTORY

| Room | Item | Give | Sell | Dispose | Specifics |
|------|------|------|------|---------|-----------|
|      |      |      |      |         |           |
|      |      |      |      |         |           |
|      |      |      |      |         |           |
|      |      |      |      |         |           |
|      |      |      |      |         |           |
|      |      |      |      |         |           |
|      |      |      |      |         |           |
|      |      |      |      |         |           |
|      |      |      |      |         |           |

An inventory taking can be partnered with sorting and decluttering. Inventory taking can be done in long hand or with the use of photography.

Create and follow a formula that works for you. Be consistent:

- Top to bottom.

- Left to right.
- Outside to inside.

Table 6

## BASIC OUTLINE OF PREMISES TO BE DOWNSIZED — 1ST WALK THROUGH AND AROUND

1. Take a walk around the home outside
2. Take a walk around the premises inside room by room.
3. Visually scan the belongings in that room.
4. Take photos or make a list of the contents (inventory).
5. Room by room and space by space commence decluttering, sorting in a consistent pattern so if you are disrupted, you can return to the task , or you can easily describe and delegate to another.

| Premises | Approximate Size (sq. ft /sq. m.) | |
|---|---|---|
| House | | |
| Apartment | | |
| Other | | |
| No. of Storeys | | |
| No of Rooms | | |
| Room Breakdown | Description | Closets |
| Bedroom 1 | | |
| Bedroom 2 | | |
| Bedroom 3 | | |
| Living Room | | |
| Dining Room | | |
| Kitchen | | |
| Washrooms | | |
| Storage | | |
| Attic | | |
| Basement/Crawl | | |
| Garage | | |
| Yard | | |
| Outer Buildings | | |
| Other | | |

Set aside containers labelled as

- Sell.
- Donate.
- Dispose.
- Other.

As you complete a room, empty the items sorted into a larger set of labeled containers (situated in the garage for example). Move the smaller containers into the next room. Repeat.

- Arrange a donation pick-up or schedule a day to take items to the organization.
- Arrange a disposal service or schedule a day to take items to the disposal facility.
- Arrange a cleaning service (for post cleanup) or schedule a day to clean as you go.
- Check off rooms as you complete them.

## 6.2 Initial considerations as you walk through a home

- Mentally take an inventory room by room.
- Are there too many things to list?
- Utilize a coding system (numbers or colors).
- Have a log or diary for recording items in the inventory. See the Items by Room list on the download kit included with this book to help.
- Do a photograph inventory in lieu of or to enhance a written one.
- Have two sets of heavy duty storage containers, good boxes, or bags.
- Label them "sell, donate, dispose, other"; these will be in the room with you.
- Label another set the same, and park them in an area where you can continually add to them, e.g., the garage.

Consider:

- Videos of property.
- Digital photos.

- specialty items, musical instruments, tools, CD and record collections, books.
- Recipes and recipe books.
- Crafts.
- Awards.
- Vehicles.
- Pets.
- Letters, cards, and correspondence.
- Bedding and linens.
- Other (property in trust for others).
- Lottery, sweepstake tickets.
- Stock, bond certificates.
- Family medical records.
- Gardening seeds, garden plants, wildflowers, gardening sheds.
- Patterns for clothing, furniture, other.
- Vitamins, prescriptions.
- Glasses.
- Canes and walkers.
- Collections eg. fine china, comic books, records, magazines.
- Maintenance records.
- Keys and security.
- Clothing in closets.
- Clothing in drawers.
- Toiletries.

As an experiment, try counting every single thing in the master bedroom. Are you surprised at the quantity?

How much time do your things take to maintain? How much does it cost to insure your things? How much time and attention have you given to specific things in the past month, year? What does that say to you?

If you walked into any room, and picked up just one item to represent you, what would that item be? Why?

Have you ever performed an inventory of your belongings and if so, why was this important or necessary at the time?

If you have to pay someone to do this for you, it would be costly. If a caregiver is tasked with the job, it will be time consuming.

---

Helpful Hint

Use sticky notes to note deficiencies in rooms by tagging repairs and so on. Use different colors to represent different tasks to save writing. Note what color codes mean to you on your inventory list: for example, blue = paint, pink = donate, yellow = clean.

---

Helpful Hint

Collect boxes or purchase boxes from a storage facility and leave a few flattened in each room until you are ready to start the packing. It can be overtiring to want to start a project, have to run out to find boxes and then return to the project. Have them on hand and ready to load.

---

Helpful Hint

Boxes: You can assemble them in a garage, tape them securely and, as you bring one in, bring one (properly labelled and filled) out, thereby building your inventory for removal to storage and emptying rooms in the process.

---

Questionnaire 9
## SORTING THROUGH BELONGINGS

| Item | | | |
|---|---|---|---|
| **Question** | **Why** | **Need** | **Want** |
| How often is this used/ worn, read seen or referred to? | | | |
| When was this last used? | | | |
| Is this depreciating (losing value or strength)? | | | |

| Is this appreciating (gaining value or strength)? | | | |
|---|---|---|---|
| Does this item define any part of me? | | | |
| Does this item provide a link to my past? | | | |
| Is this item integral to my future? | | | |
| Could this item be useful to another person or organization? | | | |
| Could I benefit space if it was not here? | | | |
| Could someone benefit by its acquisition? | | | |
| Is this costing me time (maintenance)? | | | |
| Is this costing me money (retention, storage) | | | |
| What does this item say about you if you were not around to explain it? | | | |
| Can this be upcycled? | | | |
| Can this be recycled? | | | |
| Can this be repurposed? | | | |

## 7. Storing and Storage Facilities

There are reasons to store belongings and a great many places to store them.

Individuals and caregivers may need to store belongings temporarily or for a long period of time. A decision to store may come from having to move, or while awaiting probate and the settling of an estate. You may consider storing belongings on your premises, in a garage or building available to put your things in, or use the premises of a friend, family member or other individuals or you may make use a commercial storage facility.

Whatever reason you are storing, you will need to have an inventory of the belongings in storage and make insurance provisions for their safeguarding. Further, you will need to plan how the belongings in storage will be organized for access. You may consider putting oldest at the back and newest or most needed or used at the front. You will want to organize heavier items lower and lighter items higher. You may use shelving to store labelled containers. Storing is an exercise in research and planning.

Here is an informative site that describes the magnitude of the self storage industry in Canada, the US and Australia and many other countries: http://www.selfstorage.org/ssa/Content/Navigation Menu/AboutSSA/FactSheet/default.htm.

We may need the services of a professional storage facility or we may use a more personal storage such as in a friend or neighbor's garage.

Research more than one storage facility. Compare prices charged against value and protection provided. Accessibility and security are important as is insurance. If finances restrict the use costly storage facility you may utilize the offer of a friend or family member to store your things as a short term compromise.

## Questionnaire 10
## STORAGE FACILITIES, SELF STORAGE QUESTIONS TO ASK

*Research more than one storage facility. Compare prices charged against value and protection provided. Accessibility and security are important as are insurances. If finances restrict the use costly storage facility you may utilize the offer of a friend or family member to store your things as a short term compromise.*

If using a storage facility, consider:

Date:

Storage facility:

Is the facility safe from environmental risk (heat and cold)?

Is there a security system?

Is there easy access?

Do you have to sign a contract?

What are payment terms and conditions? How much will this cost?

What are conditions for importing and retrieval?

What are guarantees and are they in writing?

What sizes are available and can you downsize your storage to smaller storage areas?

What are move in and move out terms?

In the event of illness, death and so on, what would happen to your belongings? What risks are there, such as awaiting probate?

Can next of kin, or approved individual, be given authority to access?

Will this give you peace of mind until you can deal with disbursement? (Weigh the benefits of storage.)

Is this an organization that appears stable? Are they listed in a business bureau or yelp ? Do they have good reviews?

Other:


If storing at a friend or family member's, consider:

Date:

Friend or family's name:

How long do you need to store your things at your friend's premises?

Are your things securely packed and identifiable as yours?

Do you have an inventory or pictures of your belongings?

Do you need to insure, add to your friend's insurance and so on?

Will you friend(s) agree to signing for the belongings in their trust?

Are your friends in a stable situation themselves such as current with their rent?

Do your friends expect compensation? If so, how much, for how long, and can you agree in writing?

Do you have access to your things? If so, what access?

If you wish to remove your belongings or have a yard sale at their premises are there regulations governing this such as condominium rules?

Why did you make this decision?

Other:

If relatives or friends have offered to store valuables, agree on a time limit. Seal, label and catalogue (inventory) your belongings. If you wish to remove your belongings or have a yard sale at their premises are there regulations governing this such as condominium rules? Take photos!

With downsizing, small changes yield big results in time saved in caring for things, and in the cost of storing.

4

# Human Resources

## 1. Know Yourself

Why is it important to know yourself and the people with whom you will be working?

When you choose you are in control, but if others choose they are. (Unless you have given them instruction and permission!)

You can relinquish all responsibility to a downsizing project, being fully dependent upon the decisions made by another, who may or may not be familiar with you, or you can manage aspects of the downsizing of your life in various ways. If you have made clear and definite directions it will be easier for others to follow instructions and to carry out tasks to your satisfaction.

Caregivers should think about "duty of care." It is a legal term, also referred to as standard of care. It is a responsibility or legal obligation of a person or organization to act in such a reasonable and cautious manner so as to not cause harm to others, their physical safety, and the safety of their property, particularly as it relates to a contract between parties. Not paying attention to duty of care could result in a lawsuit for negligence.

The following sections may help you better plan when choosing a caregiver who will assist with or provide downsizing service. Alternatively, the following sections may help a caregiver work with you in your downsizing project.

## 1.1 Know yourself

Why is it important to know yourself?

The time to make a diary or record of ourselves and our wants and needs is before we are unable to communicate or are unable to remember. You can refer to the Questionnaire 16; complete it for yourself, or give it to a caregiver who can use it to better understand you and provide more personal assistance.

Take a look at the charts and questionnaires in this chapter. Write down your answers, and date them. Put them away in a private but accessible place, so that in the event of an illness for example, a caregiver will be able to access them. These checklists will also serve as a guide to help you in your decision making.

Questionnaire 11
### KNOW YOURSELF

Name:

DOB:

What are your normal daily rituals? Breakfast, lunch, dinner? Exercise regime?

Are you a morning, afternoon or evening person?

Do you prefer clutter or minimalism?

Favorite color?

Preferred styles?

Do you prefer to work alone or with others? Would you rather follow instructions or lead?

Are you an introvert or extrovert?

Are you able to communicate well verbally and in writing?

Do you find making decisions difficult? Do you have someone to help you make decisions?

Do you have a support network? If so, who are they and how do they support you?

Friends (make a list with telephone numbers)

Family (make a list with telephone numbers)

Community (make a list with telephone numbers)

What inspires you, makes you happy, smile or laugh? What takes away your inspiration, makes you sad?

Do you have health or mobility challenges?

What hobbies can you take with you?

What motivates you?

Describe challenges: Transportation? Finances? Family and friends?

Are you a producer or a procrastinator?

Where do you see yourself in 1, 5, and 10 years?

Other:

It may have been a long time since you sat down and actually gave you and your situation some thought enough to write down the information. Once you have written down items on this chart, you can reflect on what challenges you face and then attempt to find solutions to work with and/or overcome them.

Taking time to reflect on and make a note of who you are and what makes you tick will take out the mystery and reduce the stress out of future decision making by yourself or a caregiver. This questionnaire should be one of the first things you do and it should be updated yearly if possible.

If you have items on this list which will cause you challenges that stop you from doing things on your own, you can research professionals and professional organizations to help you.

If you have prepared this list, you are able to discuss your intentions and this project with caregivers or advisors who will be providing assistance, such as your lawyer, accountant, financial advisor, caregiver, family member, or other service provider, and help you break down your needs into smaller, more manageable, and financially identifiable areas; e.g., what you can do on your own versus what you will need to pay for, or make arrangements for.

There are trained professionals such as counselors who can assist you with knowing yourself, your motivations, and what drives you to do the things you do if you need help completing the list.

When you pick up an item and are contemplating whether to part with it or not, you may use your own know yourself guide to take you past the indecision. For example, you might hold a china figurine in your hand admiring it, as it is beautiful and was valued through the years, but it was work maintaining its condition and you decided that after downsizing your future life would be one of minimalism. Referring to the thought you gave in making your Know Yourself questionnaire that going forward you preferred minimalism helps you put that item in the pile of things to sell or donate.

If you become incapacitated, it will serve as a guide to a caregiver as to what things you valued. For example, a caregiver can attend to your premises while you are in the hospital and select items to bring to you as he or she will be able to read what you wrote. If a downsize is required, he or she can proceed to pack up items using your Know Yourself questionnaire as a guide.

The sooner you have a completed questionnaire, the better, but it is better late than never.

What is your Style? It is good to think about this in partnership with the Know Yourself questionnaire.

Do you like historical things; wood furniture, framed photos, cluttered spaces? Do you prefer contemporary style such as mixed furniture from various sources? Do you prefer modern minimalism? No one knows you like you do.

I was given fine china as wedding gifts and on each anniversary friends and family added to the collection. Although appreciative of the value and generosity, silently I was, and always have been, a pottery person. I know this about myself.

Have your tastes evolved, and does your home does not reflect that? Would you consider a change by selling and using the proceeds from the sale to purchase new things or for a makeover?

Not unlike the purpose of your Know Yourself questionnaire, Table 8 could get you thinking about documenting and communicating things about you that may be needed by a caregiver.

## Table 7
## RITUALS AND HABITS

| Make your own list of rituals and habits | | | |
|---|---|---|---|
| Daily Rituals | Weekly Rituals | Monthly Rituals | Annual Rituals |
| walk dog | go to library | dinner and theatre with friends | travel south |
| yoga | go to church | chocolate treat | vacation |
| foods you like | salads | go to theatre | family — 3 weeks |
| music you enjoy | classical CBC | go to movie | attend seasonal concert |
| television you watch | comedy | Other: | Other: |
| Other: | Other: | | |

## Table 8
## SUPPORT NETWORKS

| Make your own list of support networks. | | | | |
|---|---|---|---|---|
| | Family | Friends | Service Providers | Counselor or Advisor |
| Who? | son / daughter | Jane, Tom, Dick | ABC Co. | Pastor Jones Ms. Brown, counsellor |
| Where? | city/away | next city, next door | city | church high school |
| Other: | | | | |

Table 9
## CHALLENGES

| Challenges — physical, mental, other (for example, finances) | | | |
|---|---|---|---|
| Daily Challenges | Weekly Challenges | Monthly Challenges | Annual Challenges |
| Time | | | |
| Transportation | | | |
| Making dinner | | | |
| Walking dog | | | |
| Other: | | | |
| Other: | | | |
| Other: | | | |
| Other: | | | |

When did you last enjoy hobby and inspiration time?

Table 10
## HOBBIES AND INSPIRATIONS

| Hobbies and Inspirations | | | |
|---|---|---|---|
| Daily | Weekly | Monthly | Annual |
| | | | |
| | | | |
| | | | |
| | | | |

# 2. Know Your Service Provider or Caregiver

If you are planning on helping someone else downsize, offer help within your limitations, whether your relationship to the person is personal or professional! You may offer a friend or family member your assistance out of a genuine desire to help, but downsizing is an enormous task fraught with many surprises and challenges. It is a stressful and emotional project. Sometimes, it is more valuable to find professional help that it is to carry out the task ourselves.

Be aware that having to quit a project due to differences of opinion could cause a relationship breakdown, so careful thought must be given to providing help, and discussions and questions should be asked or had at the onset regarding expectations. Due to possible conflict issues, not enough time, too much work, or difficult work, consider that maintaining the relationship or friendship may be more important that doing the physical task. In that case you may offer to assist in selecting an individual or a company to provide the services needed. Your help may be as simple as providing occasional meals or rides, collecting containers, taking things to recycling, and just listening over a cup of coffee or tea.

Questionnaire 12
## KNOW YOUR SERVICE PROVIDER OR CAREGIVER

Date:

Do you have a caregiver or use a service provider?

Why do you want one? Why do you feel you need one?

Where is a good place to find one? Have you checked:

- yellow pages advertisement
- referral from professional, friend
- Internet advertisements
- community centre referral or listing
- spiritual organization referral or listing

Will they agree to a fact finding meeting? Attitude is important as you will be working closely.

How professional is their demeanor, phone message, advertisement?

Are they timely and do they take notes upon meeting with you?

Do they show an interest in you, your premises?

Do they "ask" or do they "tell" ? Does this suit your need and personality?

Is the person you meet also the one who will be performing or supervising the task?

Do they offer suggestions?

What is their insurance situation? For example are they bondable? Are they complying with regulations such as insuring their workers?

What guarantees are offered? Are the guarantees in writing?

Do they provide a fee schedule and time estimates?

Do they offer a network of resources for tasks they are unable to complete (a Plan B)

If there is more than one service provider/care giver, can you interview each and choose one who suits your needs and personality as this is a highly personal task?

Other:

What should you look for when obtaining downsizing services or caregiving services? The questions in Questionnaire 17 are intended to bring attention to the fact that we need to understand the abilities and limitations of caregivers who may be performing downsizing tasks. There are excellent people molding this industry in a responsible way, and others who are unaware of the magnitude of a downsize job.

If there is more than one service provider/caregiver, can you interview each and choose one who suits your needs and personality as this is a highly personal task?

Is getting a caregiver or service provider a recommendation by a health professional, and do you agree with the recommendation? Why or why not?

Do you have the financial resources for a private caregiver or service provider?

Would a friend or family member bring more comfort than a stranger?

## 2.1 Finding a downsizing service provider

Look in the Yellow Pages or online under headings such as "transitions," "moving," "downsizing," or "relocating." Check with a community center, hospice, or support organization for recommendations. A search online for words such as downsize, relocation, transition and seniors yields results. Some individuals and companies are advertising in Senior magazines, such as http://www.seniorlivingmag.com/ magazine and organizations offering training and designations such as http://www.crtscertification.com will provide referrals to individuals and companies by area, as well as Professional Organizers , http://www.organizersincanada.com/about/ Many of these companies list their codes of ethics which are worth a read.

As so many of the downsizers are individuals as yet, they are often functioning on a referral basis. They have visited organizations such as local health authorities, hospices, and estate lawyers to introduce themselves so a large advertising presence is not merited and thus they are not highly visible.

Listings for more than one in a jurisdiction indicates that there is a need for the service advertised and indicates use by others, thereby available references are a likelihood. (Call them, speak to them.) If the service provider is new to this, find out how and why he or she is doing this and decide what the value of these guarantees are to you. You may choose to have the work supervised by a family member, lawyer, or so on. If you are electing to downsize yourself and wish for professional help or personal organization companies and businesses, you can research professional memberships and certifications with the growing needs for senior assistance. For example, in Canada, an individual with a CRTS designation is a certified relocation and transition specialist (CRTS is a designation awarded to Senior Transition Specialists who meet experience and eligibility exam requirements). An individual or business registered with the Better Business Bureau might also be contacted.

## 3. Downsizing Advisors: Pulling a Team Together

The importance of putting together a team of advisors is to provide advice, support, and guidance to assist you in decision making. As the job of downsizing grows, so will possible situations arise that need addressing, quite often immediately. if you have prepared a list of advisors with whom you are familiar and whose advice you trust, you will be able to refer to the list, or someone representing you will be able to make a call, make an appointment, and have your questions answered or attended to in a timely fashion and the advisor will know why they are on the list and have some background on your situation.

Not unlike having a "person to contact in case of emergency" list posted on your fridge or in your diary, you should consider putting together your "downsize team" list and keeping it updated and accessible.

The practice of having a list prepared is beneficial in preparing or dealing with the unforeseen and the unplanned in a timely and effective manner. A crisis situation is not the time to have to start hiring advisors, such as lawyers, accountants, and the others on the list. You may consider giving each of your team members a copy of the list so they are familiar with each other, but that is a personal decision.

## 3.1 Your team

The following is a suggested list of the people who will make up your initial support network. There is more about team members in Chapter 4 (Human Resources) and Chapter 7 (Service Providers, Caregivers, and Advisors):

- Lawyers
- Accountants
- Financial advisors
- Physician
- Veterinarian
- Bankers
- Realtors
- Counselors
- Spiritual advisors
- Community support workers
- Realtor
- Home insurer
- Downsizing service provider
- Caregiver
- Storage companies

Remember when choosing downsizing team members you need to be able to access them, and be able to understand their instructions. Caregivers may be are individuals or employees of companies that provide a service for a fee or as a volunteer to assist in moving and dealing with the belongings of individuals.

They may help:

- Coordinate details of moving, such as packing in preparation for relocating to a senior facility
- Move someone from a larger home to a smaller residence.
- Assist in selling or disposing of your belongings.
- Handle cleaning up and selling or disposing of an estate.

- Arrange packers and movers.

- Make plans, coordinate, and facilitate moves for special needs.

- Clean and prepare items for selling including inventory taking.

- Advertise the sale of belongings in newspapers, flyers, email, and regular mail-outs, street signs, estate sales, garage sales and other community notices or periodicals.

- Offer counseling if qualified to do so.

Some may hold professional designations while others are well meaning volunteers or individuals making a living offering services.

It is an emerging industry, and many are advertising their services, so do your research, interview, check references and read contracts and agreements and consider the validity of guarantees.

Some examples of individuals or organizations offering downsizing services are listed in magazines, community support brochures, telephone books, newspapers and periodicals, and online.

---

Helpful Hint

Well-meaning friends or relatives might not be able to complete the job. They may not be able to do it physically or they may lack the time needed. They may simply not want to do a downsizing job. Have a backup plan of a professional downsizing services you can call. Let the downsizing service provider quoting you or consulting with you know that they are a backup unless you do decide to use them.

---

# 5

# Stress Management

## 1. Downsizing and Stress

There is a world of stress related to downsizing.

Even if the downsize was planned for a positive transitioning, and often it is not, there are emotions relating to feelings of nostalgia, loss, or change of the familiar, and a disorientation period as an individual moves from an accumulation phase to disposal phase in life.

There will be the adjustment from established routines to new routines, particularly if the act of downsizing is a process that has not been routinely practiced or was sudden. There are physical stresses associated with increased activity, and there are mental stresses with all the decision making. There may be stresses associated with worrying about an ill person and his or her care, or thinking about a deceased person and all that is required in final arrangements, and there are stresses with possibly having to deal with strangers in the eliminating of belongings.

There are things an individual can do such as ensuring his or her physician or other health providers are informed, or utilizing a professional or company that handles tasks which cannot be easily handled by the individual.

Take care of your physical and emotional needs. Take instruction and direction from your health care provider(s).

- Join a support network of others in a similar age group or situation.
- Accept assistance and listen to advice from advisors before making decisions.
- Ask for help.
- Stay in communication with other empathetic individuals.

There is a tremendous amount of emotion, ranging from shock to fear, annoyance and dread, to anger and resentment, to elation and often ever-present disorganization and confusion when dealing with a downsizing situation. What I heard myself saying time and again was how I wished it all was in a book, a guide, something to take me forward from step one, and most importantly to recognize what step one was. As it turned out, there were many step ones, often occurring concurrently. Had I known then what I know now, life would have been much easier, the stresses better handled, the values of goods better achieved, and services for assisting individuals more wisely selected. It was a lesson a day, or so it seemed; checklists grew from daily to-do lists to elaborate and detailed plans. There is still work required on emotional closure after the physical work is done, but that is a subject for those trained in that field, those who hopefully will tackle the subject in a simple, instructive manner. The absence of help can mean a great deal of added stress to caregivers, as can be read in books such as *The 36-Hour Day* by Nancy L. Mace and Peter V. Rabins (Grand Central Publishing, 2001).

## 2. Prioritize Tasks

Prioritizing tasks can help you get through a stressful situation one item at a time.

Let's imagine friend or family member has taken ill and is incapacitated. You get a call from the hospital to come as you have been listed as an emergency contact. The person is suffering with something that requires a mask to visit, but can communicate. He hands you a fist full of keys and asks you to take care of his place as there is no one else responding or available. It is unknown how dire his health situation is, and his home had been abandoned for several days (or weeks). The date he will go home from the hospital is unknown. You have been given keys, none of them identified as to what they belong to, some instruction, and permission to give help. You commence by taking care of the home, but then discover that the individual will not be able to continue to live independently and a move to a care facility is the next step.

You must manage your stress in this situation, and consider the physical and emotional toll while trying to perform many tasks simultaneously.

As you are attending to the enormous and overwhelming task of cleaning out the home of someone who has taken ill and will not be going back to his or her home, there are things which need to be done.

1. Plan your own home's routine first (prepare food in a slow cooker, etc). Ensure you have any time off work, daycare, or pet care needed, etc. ("Etc." can be a task in itself!)

2. Schedule the day ahead of you.

3. Ensure your vehicle is filled with gas (there will likely be a lot of driving). Keep a diary or log to record kilometers and miles driven for that purpose. Keep gas receipts. Log times in and times out.

4. Have a personal travel bag equipped with pen(s), paper, flashlight, cell phone, keys to premises, and practical and professional advisors to call list. Not unlike emergency numbers posted on the fridges of households everywhere, we should have a downsizing emergency list in the event we are called to talk, or if the downsize is for ourselves.

5. Bring nutritious food and drink for yourself.

6. Bring a notepad to write what needs to be done, and check off what was done.

7. Bring lots of garbage bags, storage containers, boxes, a flashlight, and good quality rubber gloves.

8. Have a basic first aid kit in your vehicle, and a change of clothes.

9. Have a bucket with cleaning products such as baking soda, vinegar, scrubbers, clean cloths, and paper towels in trunk in case you need it.

Once you arrive, attend to the premises and check what needs to be done on your notepad:

1. Do an outside walk-around to check for any problems (e.g., leaks, broken windows , etc.).

2. Does the grass need cutting? Do you need a landscaping service? Check the hoses. Is the water turned on or off?

3. Collect the mail (check that key ring for a key!)

4. Move newspapers and flyers away from entrances and mailboxes.

5. Remove cobwebs, leaves from entranceways, etc.

6. Note whether outside lights are on and if timer is functioning properly.

7. Bring garbage containers in from street.

If there appear to be problems ( e.g., attempted entry) do not enter and seek immediate help. If you do not see any immediate issues, enter the premises, and secure doors behind you. Attend to these priority things first:

1. If you have a check-in person (friend or spouse) make the call upon entry.

2. Walk through the premises listening for sounds (TV, radio, a possible animal, e.g., mice) and attend to the source.

3. Attend to smells (garbage needing emptying, food decomposing on counters).

4. Check appliances such as fridge for spoiling food, stove for food left cooked in pots or otherwise, washer and dryer for wet clothes.

5. Check bathrooms (toilets needing flushing, and other shockers).

6. Check bedrooms for soiled bedding, and strip beds for cleaning and airing out.

7. Check garages, woodsheds, crawlspaces, and storage areas to see what condition they are in, and look for a cleaned area to start a sorting process (a place to put garbage containers and recycling).

8. Check windows, doors, closets and storage areas, particularly in the homes of forgetful or distressed individuals, for anything unusual.

As you go from room to room, try to get an idea of the overall condition. Take notes which will make up your to-do list.

1. Turn on every light including lamps as you enter a room or area. Note and attend to broken fixtures.

2. Check for soiled carpets, floors, or furniture.

3. If you will be using a cleaning service, you will have an idea of what needs to be done to communicate that to the professionals. If you are not able to use a cleaning service, you will have started your to-do checklist. Assess whether you need a rodent control service.

The ill resident may be returning, so initially it may be a cleanup. A big cleanup. If the ill resident is not to return, the downsize scenario will likely commence. If the ill resident does return, and did not have a downsize plan, consider compiling one before for the next emergency, particularly if there are health issues.

Take a break each hour as you work. Assess your progress, and make updates to your to-do list.

Try to find a current address book (e.g., to call legal representatives as needed, friends, family, services, other). Collect mail, put it in a secure area, but do not open it unless authorized to do so. You can scan for past due notices to avoid a possible disconnection of utilities.

If there is a problem it will have to be addressed. If you are not authorized to make payments on behalf of someone else, or cannot pay, call the utility and explain the situation, and ask for guidance from the ill person's legal representative.

Start slowly, a few hours a day if you are not used to this. You can increase the time spent taking care of things when you are able.

Do a walk-through as you leave the premises, taking notes to prepare your next to-do list so you don't forget items to be done. Use a digital camera to help remind yourself of the condition of the home, and to assemble your next to-dos.

Remember to:

- Turn off lights.

- Secure windows and doors.

- If neighbors are receptive, introduce yourself and see if they can keep you informed of any issues that may need your attention.

- Put garbage out for removal or take to a garbage disposal unit. Recyclables can wait.

- Clean up, change your clothing.

- Prepare to summarize the day, make phone calls, appointments, and take care of your own business.

## 3. Visit the Person Who Trusts You to Deal with His or Her Belongings

When visiting an ill person, provide assurances of the things that are under your control. Do not burden an ill person with the drama of the tasks, or problems, as this will add to their stress of being away from home and being ill or incapacitated. Caregivers provide comfort. If you need to know things, ask, for example, "Do you have a downsize plan, and where is it? Do you have a good friend or neighbor, and who is it?"

Ask whether there is anything you can do, or if he or she needs anything. Enquire about pet issues. Enquire about legal representation in case you need to do more (you will need legal permission and authority, presumably from a person appointed as power of attorney. A lawyer may not be able to discuss anything with you under a duty of confidentiality, but you can inform the lawyer of your concerns and provide details for their action and direction. Always keep good receipts, notes, and records).

Take direction from health professionals attending to him or her. How is he or she progressing, and what is the estimated date he or she will return home? If he or she will be returning, you will be needed to prepare the premises for a return. This could include a grocery shopping trip the day before. Schedule any other services needed, such as yard maintenance, cleaning services, etc., that you are authorized to do. Be prepared to share details of all you have done in his or her absence with him or her, or other interested parties.

If he or she will not be returning, connect with advisors and proceed with legal permission and direction to proceed. Proceeding may mean a total cleanup, downsize, home listing, tax preparation, banking, or perhaps nursing home placement. Be prepared as these can be very large tasks even when legal permissions are in place; a lot of this will need legal approval (e.g., you being named power of attorney or executor, or the power of attorney or executor giving you permission) before you can move ahead.

Take good physical and emotional care of yourself. Seek assistance, care, and advice. This task is best carried out as part of an evolving to-do list. Plans will come as unknowns are eliminated. You could be dealing with many unknowns, so the best you can do is be prepared for what you can do to the best of your ability.

For those reading this who have not made downsize plans for themselves, the above and more is what a friend or relative will face if you take ill and do not have any plans in order.

Traversing the legal map is difficult enough with measures in place, so take another step and get your downsizing plans in place. Give trusted people the information they will need to make decisions to help you.

- Attend to a power of attorney.

- Attend to a representation agreement.

- Attend to a will.

- Attend to a downsize plan for your possessions today.

# 4. Communication

Communication is important. Without communication we cannot express our needs, or offer or receive appropriate help. Problems either take longer to solve or do not get solved at all.

When asking for assistance or giving instruction, ask the individual with whom you are interacting what they understand you have said. Hear it in their own words. Were you understood? If not, make efforts to rephrase in a meaningful way, inviting their input. If that is not working, you need to find someone to help you communicate.

Ask questions and listen for the answers. Do not simply tell or make an assumption of knowledge. This is particularly important between a caregiver and a recipient of the service. Showing and explaining is more meaningful when facing a communication breakdown. A head shake doesn't always mean understanding. Avoid closed-ended questions ("Do you want the upstairs packed today?") Opt instead for open-ended questions ("What do you want packed upstairs today? Can you show me so that I am clear on your instruction?")

Alternatively a receiver of the service can opt for "Will you describe how you will move my things?" over the closed-ended "Will you move my things for me?"

## 4.1 Barriers to Communication and How to Overcome Them

Sometimes communication barriers can cause stress; here are some ways to overcome that.

- Language differences: Consider an interpreter or a multilingual individual; if the issue is technology, try using an individual who can explain simply.

- Cultural differences: Consider an interpreter or a peer of the individual.

- Gender bias or stereotyping: Be prepared to provide proof of expertise or credentials, testimonials, or assurances. Ask if there is any possibility for an accommodation to be made based on merit. If you are a paying client and experience a problem, consider requesting another individual with whom communication would be more effective.

- Distances: If you are awaiting instruction or approvals from someone in another time zone, e.g., a vacationing client, or the next of kin of an individual receiving service or care and time is of the essence, like the requirement for an approval on a bid on an auction item, the lag in time due to distance could cause the loss of a sale. Have a backup plan for dealing with people and situations at a distance.

- Technology and education: Technology is a useful tool and medium for marketing items for sale and for documenting histories. It is highly specialized and words and terms can mean different things. It is best to work with individuals who will provide examples of what can be accomplished.

- Unclear motivation: If something is a favor, it should remain a favor. If a situation changes, discuss why a favor can no longer continue, expressing clearly the reasons why. For example in advertising, question promises made, e.g., examine the offer and ask for clarity. Using a mission statement in advertising helps the readers know what the intentions are. If you are calling an advisor for assistance, state the specific reason for the need for information.

- Unclear reward: If an individual is expecting to receive compensation for work performed it should be clear to all parties at the onset so as to avoid conflicts. A reward should be defined.

- Lack of feedback: Progress should be communicated throughout the downsize job. "I like how this is going," or "I hope this can be improved as soon as possible," so that behavior or actions do not result in a continuation of an activity which many not yield positive results to the mutual benefit of all parties.

- Lack of empathy: Not everyone shares empathy for a given situation. One can counter the lack of empathy received (or needed) using trained professionals to complete a task. Agree to a plan, obtain and share feedback, discuss problems and solutions as they occur. Work with what you have. Acknowledge another's situation, but keep the end task in view. Stay positive. Try communicating concerns and sensitive issues with a friend, manager, or advocate. Do not personalize another's actions.

- Lack of appropriate training: Seek out training needed to perform a job appropriately, upgrade your skills regularly, delegate to a more experienced individual, the sooner the better; consider subcontracting to a more appropriate party.

- Lack of patience: Try to understand why you need patience with a situation or individual. If the problem is as a result of a lack of time, you can consider hiring extra help. If the problem is a problematic individual, consider assigning the task or individual to another.

- Timing: Consider using support or additional help. Explain the problems with the timeline and request an extension. Revisit time allotments; can more time be made by rearranging breaks?

# 5. Respect

RESPECT: (Noun)

A feeling of deep admiration for someone or something elicited by their abilities, qualities, or achievements.

What does respect have to do with downsizing? A great deal, actually. As we take control of our lives, we practice self respect and garner respect and admiration from those who see us live or work in an efficient and worthwhile way. As we downsize we are able to provide evidence of our abilities to make good, sound, and beneficial choices about how we wish for our belongings to be treated and received, and in how we communicate our lives and our wishes through the disbursement of our belongings. It is often through our outward appearances and the belongings we display that others know something about us, otherwise it is easy to become just another face in a crowd. How you portray yourself to the world and the control you maintain as sound decisions are made is a first step in garnering respect. How you treat others, even in the face of adversity — particularly in the face of adversity. How you bounce back can mean more than how you fall. Sometimes the challenges of life make people more quiet and withdrawn or combative and angry, and yet a life long and well-lived deserves to be shared for the benefit of others.

Showing respect is not giving away anything. Giving respect speaks volumes of good things about the giver.

What does respect have to do with downsizing? You will be dealing with a generation of persons where showing respect to an elder was a given. You may be dealing with a generation of persons who, through their hard work, will be providing you with a very personal service.

You can respect that an individual comes from an era when good manners were part of life.

When you show respect, you are not giving anything away, What you are is setting an example of courtesy which sets a tone also for how you wish to be treated.

When in doubt:

- Refer to an individual as Mr., Mrs., or Ms. unless otherwise directed.
- Use "please" and "thank you."
- Listen before speaking, and speak loudly enough to be heard, but quietly enough to be respectful.
- Ask permission, even when presented with the obvious. "Do you mind if I go on a walk-through of your home? Do you mind if I take notes? Do you mind if I take photos?" Show, then tell.
- Give a genuine compliment. Find something positive to say about the situation, the person, or even the weather.
- Ask questions and wait for the answers.
- If you are insulted, it may be an individual's inability to understand common courtesy or a language problem, or a mental condition. Do not engage the individual, but rather ask them to please explain what they mean.
- If you are in a confrontational situation, remove yourself politely from the situation, and give yourself and them a cool-down period.
- Think of how you wish for this situation to conclude or proceed. If you agree to revisit a situation, keep your promise of a time and date.

Although there appears to be a lack of mutual respect between generations, it may be more of a lack of meaningful dialogue. Generations have become isolated from one another, in part due to technology and the differences in meanings of words and in a world where so many people are rushing to and from work and taking care of families and expenses.

Successful partnering of generations can embrace the notion of cooperation and reciprocity; each possessing and offering something the other needs. Elders may be able to economically and emotionally contribute to supporting the efforts, time, and attention provided by youth, and youth can support the elders in contemporary ways by paying attention and attending to the well-being of the elderly with tasks or assisting in matters of a physical nature, or of an academic or intellectual nature, such as assisting with technology or providing physical services.

Communicating with each other and trying to bridge a communication gap is a worthy task. The meanings of words have changed and elders may not understand what is being said. You don't know what you don't know. Remember, once upon a time, a web was something spiders made, not the Internet.

Youthful interpretation coupled with elderly wisdom is a dynamic coupling. Alternatively, there may be elders who have been able to remain abreast of technology, but underprivileged youth have not had the opportunity or the economics to indulge. In that case, the roles can still complement one another as each seeks to share each other's strengths and bridge weaknesses.

Elders, be conscious of youth, and youth, reach out to elders. You can be a strong team together. Embrace reciprocity.

How caregivers can show respect and good manners:

1. Don't launch into conversation without saying hello and introducing yourself. When returning a call, for example, Ask if the time is convenient and give the reason for your call.

2. Ask, don't tell.

3. Show, then tell (as in instruction).

4. Acknowledge what the person said and reaffirm his or her question or concern.

5. Advise politely if you are taking notes or recording and what you intend to do with the notes or recording.

6  Use "please" and "thank you."

7. Use eye contact and a respectful manner.

8. Remove outdoor shoes and boots and wear shoe or boot covers. (These can be purchased as they are often worn by tradespeople.)

9. If in someone's home, ask him or her to please lead.

10. Always ask permission to enter, to proceed, to contact a person, and so on.

11. Maintain a high standard of confidentiality.

12. Maintain a high standard of privacy and security.

13. Treat others as you wish to be treated.

# 6. Help: Asking and Offering

Asking for help is not everyone's favorite activity. There is the fear of rejection and there is the fear of others seeing you as vulnerable or needy. Asking for help is actually courageously making an effort to help oneself.

If the answer is no, you are no further behind than if you didn't ask at all, and you can broaden your request to others, such as your professional advisors. It is good to know that even helpful individuals may have to refuse to assist due to personal circumstances.

Sometimes humor helps break up an uncomfortable situation (especially with someone who refused to help you). In seeing a person after a failed attempt to get help, you can address the matter with humor, such as, "Are you sure you don't have a Saturday to spare for some carrot cake, or maybe your kids, or that handsome Uncle Joe?" Try to remain positive and not mind the perceived slight.

If the answer is yes, you can ask when a good time would be to get together and schedule times and duties and means of compensation.

On the flip side, perhaps you want to offer to help an individual who may be too proud or shy to request assistance. You see someone struggling with heavy containers day after day and know that he or she may appreciate a helping hand.

Offering help can offend someone who is too proud or independent and doesn't want to admit frailty or vulnerability.

Consider "You want help?" versus "I was wondering if there was something I could do for you. I am going to the recycling center, is there anything I can bring away for you?"

You can make a person comfortable by offering small tokens or gestures of assistance. Once you have opened the lines of communication, you can address other areas where you may be of help.

If you cannot personally assist, you may be able to help them choose others who can.

Some examples of help offers to break the ice and not commit to more than you can handle:

- Is there something I can do to help you this Saturday for a few hours?

- What have you eaten today? (as opposed to Did you eat today?)

- Would you like some company? I have a new tea that I was hoping to share with someone this weekend.

- Do you need a ride somewhere? I am free Wednesday afternoon.

- May I walk your dog on Sunday?

Examples of an unhelpful offer that does not encourage dialogue and basically does not offer anything of value: "I hope you are okay." This is rather meaningless. It does not encourage an answer or offer of help in any way. A better question would be "Is there anything you need that I can do?" This encourages communication between parties and is a genuine offer to help.

# 7. Conflict Resolution

At the onset of any task, spend time asking questions and getting answers in order to avoid potential conflict.

Use the questionnaires in this guide to address possible issues before they arise. Check with insurance companies as to rights and responsibilities and perform the tasks to the best of your ability, or get or give training in the case of those people employed in downsizing services. Own up to an error as soon as possible and be truthful about your understanding of the conflict.

If employed in a downsizing capacity, understand who you are to report problems to, and when. Asking as opposed to telling will take you a long way to understanding what you are dealing with. Resolve early.

Discuss boundaries, and who does what and when.

1. Make your needs and wishes clear, communicate.

2. Set boundaries for yourself and know your goal or objective.

3. Accept another's boundaries.

4. Ask questions.

5. Keep copies of contracts, signed documents, and notes taken during conversations.

6. Explain yourself and listen equally to explanations by others.

7. Use a mediator or advocate.

8. Know yourself (remember the questionnaires in Chapter 4).

9. Meet with advisors ahead of the task to gain their advice and input.

10. Network with like-minded people who can relate to your situation, talk about shared concerns and strategies, and so on.

11. Consider joining a support network of others in a similar age group or situation.

12. Accept assistance and listen to advice from advisors before making decisions.

13. Ask for help.

14. Stay in communication with another skilled, trained, or empathetic individual.

If a conflict arises, for example an argument or a difference of opinion, identify the nature of the conflict.

Is it about what to do with belongings, why a price was not achieved, or how something was broken or damaged? Get all sides and versions of the event equally and try to mitigate the loss of the downsizing job or depreciation of the relationship by seeking a resolution, utilizing a mediator in the event of a breakdown in communication, or utilizing an advisor.

In downsizing, stuff is going to happen and tempers are going to flare, as people are tired, confused, and often disorganized. It is more than just showing up at a friend's place and packing boxes, although that is okay provided that was understood.

Imagine someone can help you pack boxes on Saturday, but shows up and nothing is inventoried or ready, and some boxes are in a room along with tape. There are no real instructions. Things get packed and taped and then someone walks in the room and asks where things are, and a job needs to be redone. Your helper is upset at the useless time spent, and other people are upset that this person didn't get it. The first person decides that the favor is becoming more stressful than anticipated and is busy the following Saturday. The person who needs help is in a lurch. The two cease speaking.

This conflict could have been avoided with a proper plan in place, and understanding of who does what and how, and who is the one who makes the ultimate decision.

It would have gone better if:

Person A showed up to help Person B (paid or otherwise), but then Person B showed Person A what was to be done and they agreed on what was expected before the commencement of the tasks. It would be done to the satisfaction of Person B, and all parties would have left that day knowing a job/task was done as required and directed. Each party would have understood the motivation, the task, and the expectations because they were clearly communicated.

# 6

# Belongings and How to Deal with Them

Easy does it: Think of getting rid of belongings as liberation, not loss.

## 1. Where Should All These Things Go?

If you are too emotional about the disposal of belongings, you may consider storing your things for a set time period until you are in a frame of mind conducive to dealing with the issue.

Consider renting a well-insured storage locker for a year and on a monthly or quarterly visit to the storage, slowly relinquish the items in priority sequence of oldest and least used to most currently used, and "wish to replace" or " time to go to ... "

Out of sight, out of mind, and you may discover that the sentiment of the item which once held great meaning or helped you define yourself is no longer needed. You may come to realize that the memory of an individual, time, or place is more important than taking care of a souvenir of it. Perhaps you have made even better memories in the years since the reminder item has been out of sight.

You may just hang on to it a bit longer and deal with it another year or meet someone worthy of a gift and a good story to accompany it.

Or, you may decide to throw a friends and family lottery, as described later in this chapter.

---

Helpful Hint

Consider taking art apart when offering it for sale if it does not damage it, or separating art from the frame. Often people will buy something for either the picture or the frame, but get both in the process. By separating some pictures from their frames, you may attain more sale value from a piece of art that looks better out of an undated frame, or from a valuable frame not housing a undesirable piece of art.

---

## Table 11
## PROBLEMS AND SOLUTIONS

| Problem | Possible Solutions |
|---|---|
| Friends and family are unavailable to assist 100% | Consider engaging a service provider or caregiver for the work that they cannot do. |
| Value of belongings is unknown. | Research or have an individual with knowledge and expertise do research for you. Take advice from an organization experienced with valuations. Ask your insurance adjuster for advice. If the problem is encountered by a service provider seek direction from the owner or manager |
| Two or more prospective beneficiaries want an item, a one of a kind item of value. | Yikes! Tough one! Consider selling the item and split the proceeds among the beneficiaries. |
| Limited income for hiring help. | Consider a contra arrangement where a provider is willing to exchange service fees for an item or a percentage of the sales of belongings. Be sure to obtain any agreements in writing. |
| Items of no monetary value but great sentimental value. | One of the toughest situations to deal with. Each must deal with it in his/her own way. Make a decision and then live with it without regret. |

| What happens if any item is damaged or broken by you | Admit guilt. Take responsibility and seek a resolution for reimbursement with insurer, or come to a compromise between parties. With the advice of a solicitor or other relevant advisor, agree in writing that the matter has been resolved and the manner in which it has been resolved. |
|---|---|
| Broken promise or unfulfilled contract or agreement | Take instruction from a solicitor as to the best way to proceed. There may be the desire to make restitution, a partial or total reimbursement, a reduction in fees , or offer to assist in finding another to complete the tasks. As this could be a litigious situation involve legal advisor as soon as possible. |
| Other: | |

Helpful Hint

Put jewelry bits, e.g., collections of single earrings, into a baggie with a picture of something that could be made with them. This is called repurposing. This may make what you are selling more appealing to crafty or DIY people.

## 2. Marketing in Order to Sell

After you have researched and selected the items to be sold, some marketing is going to be needed so that you can attract a buyer to you. You can simply throw everything into a garage sale, but you won't get the best prices for your things. Whether you are doing this for yourself, or you are a caregiver doing this for someone else, you need to dedicate time to the designing of ads, selecting where to advertise, who you are appealing to, when the best time to advertise and how you will do this.

Be strategic and relative. There is no point selling a designer purse at an auction for tools! Consider who you think your purchaser would be and design an ad that appeals to that group. This is called targeting your market.

There is ease in the placing of an online ad. It is not only fast but has a great market reach owing to the number of people who are connected and the lack of geographical boundaries.

For example, if you are hoping to attract the eye (and the contents of the wallet) of the millenial age group, know that they are communicating and conversing in places like Facebook, Instagram, Twitter and Kijiji to name a few with brevity, speed and witticisms. Your ad design for this demographic could easily take the simplified look of "great furniture, mint, make an offer" written on a snapshot and posted online.

---

Helpful Hint:

You may want to check words used in descriptions in the Urban Dictionary online, to ensure you have not committed a faux pas in word selection and find you have used urban slang, unless it suits the purpose.

---

Use attractive pictures to showcase your belongings. Use descriptive words (and #hashtags). Instructions on how to advertise are easy to follow, often just filling in some details, adding a photo, a description, your return email and hitting send.

You can quickly and easily modify an ad to expand into another demographic, or age group. The same furniture advertised above to attract the eye (and contents of the wallet) of a baby boomer in e.g. Kijiji, eBay, Buy and Sell, the classifieds, or other selling sites may need descriptions to be expanded and include more details, something along the line of "heritage furniture, quality built, well maintained, great for departing students or the grandkids," will consider reasonable offers.

Tailor the message to the medium and then get the message out there!

In addition to individuals who may be wanting or needing what you are selling, there are others who may be interested. Compose a list of businesses that you can send email notifications, together with a picture, particularly authentic retro items.

You may send an introductory letter to companies you have researched such as those who outfit movie sets, or retro restaurants and shops.

A picture does speak a thousand words; get people's attention using color instead of black and white. Use a picture of a sofa in an attractive setting near fresh flowers rather than a forlorn looking sofa in a dimly lit garage.

There's also a reason why successful companies spend so much on packaging. It's very much about the visual, or eye appeal.

Eye catching appearance helps you price your belongings more competitively. You can show functionality by showcasing it in its best light and setting.

Novelty attracts the eye. Don't be like all others.

Are you in a small or large community, rural,urban community or city? Do you have an idea of the age, ethnicity, history, culture, income brackets of the area?

Have you visited the local community website to familiarize yourself with the area?, Is the population increasing and are there many new building projects? What are your distribution challenges? Is there access to postal delivery, professional mover? Knowing your demographic helps you design effective advertisement that appeal.

With the use of a camera and few skillfully placed words you can change your ad to suit your target market easily.

## 2.1 Staging your belongings for viewing or selling

Depending on the market demographic you are wishing to appeal to, e.g., upwardly mobile professional, newcomer to the country setting up a new home, student, you should consider designing a few ads to appeal directly to that age group or consumer.

Include a description or picture or wording that directs to them exclusively

If you are selling your home, and/or its contents, you may wish to engage the services of a professional home stager. These are individuals skilled at staging homes who will (for a fee) consult, provide suggestions on how to decorate a home for prospective buyers, and even add furnishings to assist you in that goal.

The objective is to prepare a property for sale, present it in it's best light in order to achieve the best price. Research staging services and check with realtors for referrals.

# 3. Disposal

The world is a global community. One person can do a lot of damage by taking shortcuts disposing of things like chemicals, tires, electronics, etc. inappropriately. Tires should not be burned and batteries are not tossed into a lake or buried anymore, and they never should have been.

There are an increasing number of rules, regulations (and fines) regarding the disposal of chemicals and offending goods. Damage caused by air, land and water pollution has created huge environmental challenges. The cost to restore and repair damage can be infinitely great and in some cases impossible to correct. Do not be an environmental offender to save a few dollars. If you have financial challenges, ask for help to do the right thing.

There are companies that are trained, certified, and equipped to handle the removal of questionable items in a household. Check with a local waste removal company for a referral to professionals who will assess and remove questionable products and items safely.

No one may see chemicals being poured down the drain, and you may think it doesn't matter because it is an isolated incidence, but, environmental damage is cumulative. The water will know, the fish will know, and when you are eating food that you believe to be freshly caught, and you wonder why you are developing health conditions, you will know.

Everyone has to do their part responsibly.

## 3.1 Recycle and reuse

Everyone has been introduced to the concept and practice of recycling. In fact, recycling is now mandatory in most areas. We separate our garbage by material, such as plastic, glass, metal regularly and it is dealt with separately from our garbage. We get charged recycling taxes and fees when we buy items like paint or tires.

# 4. Donating

Who donates? Anyone can.

Why donate? You may decide to donate everything or some of your things if you feel that this is the best avenue for the disbursement of your belongings.

The reasons to donate can be any or all of the following:

- You wish to reward someone.
- The effort to sell may not have yielded results.

- The task may be too great.
- You do not require the money from the sale of goods.
- Others may have a greater need.
- You wish to support a charity or cause.

Some organizations offer to pick up and take away belongings and provide a tax receipt which you may choose to take advantage of.

Ask questions such as:

- What will happen to what is being donated?
- Will the benefit be local or other?
- Is this going to a non profit charity or organization or a profit making institution or individual? Are you happy to know that what you donate is a cause that you believe in or stand for?
- Does this organization practice responsibility?
- Does this organization recycle?

## 5. Benefits of Photography in Downsizing Projects

As we make downsizing decisions, we should consider that our photographs are a record of the past, and although we can purge many printed photos, there are ways and means to preserve family photos and histories for many generations to come at little to no additional cost. The following paragraphs will shed light on some of the current ways in order to preserve, display, revisit, and share our photography.

Photography was once a luxury, now most handheld devices (phones) come equipped with a camera. Digital cameras now come in many sizes and shapes and can be inexpensive to purchase.

Once costly and time consuming in reproduction (film purchase and processing), now you can see immediately the photo and share it simultaneously with as many people as you like.

Photographs allow you to work on your downsizing project: for example you can make a visual inventory or you can delegate tasks from a photo while you are away from the premises.

With photographs, and the ease of sharing, via email you can solicit advice or interest as simply as text messaging.

- Photography is a useful tool for taking inventory.
- Photography is a means of remaining connected to a time, to people, an age or era that we lived.

- Photography is a testament to who we are.

- Photography is a way to remember past belongings we have sold, donated, or passed on.

# 6. Collages

Why a collage and what is a collage? It is an assortment and arrangement of photos and other memorabilia such as awards and certificates artfully arranged to depict a theme or a character.

Collages do not take up as much space as vertical real estate. In other words, a collage hung on a wall (as opposed to items stored in storage containers away from view and interest) allows the individual to view, to reflect upon, and to demonstrate to others who an individual is and from where he or she comes.

Go through your photos, choose one or two from each year of your life. Arrange them in a way that you like. Use pins to initially attach them to a lightweight foam core board. Once you like the look, take a photo of it and share it with friends and family. Have your own mounted professionally and framed so that you take a reminder of your history with you, without the bulk of storing.

Why do a collage?

1. It's fun.

2. It's informative visually.

3. It's an acknowledgement and reminder of our lives.

4. It's a visual for ourselves and others, particularly if you are going into a care facility, but also a good exercise for anyone.

5. It's a place to consolidate your photos and you can take a picture of the finished collage to share with others interested in your family history.

---

Helpful Hint

Making collages is a great little job for a hobbyist or an aspiring artist. You can contact the local art department of a community college or post ads in hobby shops or craft stores to find if there are individuals who would like to take on a creative project either as a school project or for a fee you are prepared to pay.

---

---

Helpful Hint

Use waterproof containers; smaller boxes for heavier items. Make sure to tag, label, and date containers.

---

Helpful Hint

Use dryer sheets or strips of fabric that have been sprayed with remnants of favorite scents and perfumes and put into sock drawers, winter boots, or containers holding memorabilia. Keep dryer sheets and other deodorizers from coming into direct contact as the oils in them could damage your belongings. Always read safety labels first.

---

Helpful Hint

Invite friends and family to select photos they may wish to have after you have saved them to a DVD or CD, for example. Consider disposing of them or donating them to organizations that collect older photos.

---

# 7. Auctions

There are many avenues for the downsizing or disposing of small items such as garage sales, estate sales, buy and sells, and online sales. Disposing and getting good value for larger things such as furniture and appliances, collections and artifacts, vehicles and other large items of value require a more specialized system for selling. Using an auction (or the services of a professional auctioneer) may better suit the selling of the item, or items.

Some auction houses will provide estimates and all the advertising relating to marketing the items they are selling. They do this for a fee, which is usually a percentage of sales. Some auction houses advertise internationally and some locally promote the sale of goods and belongings.

Researching auction establishments and sending an enquiry about what you are desiring with respect to the selling of belongings will enlighten you as to what path for selling you should take.

You can send a photo or a detailed description and ask them if they feel they have a market for the sale of your item. You must ask what the fees are for appraising, transporting, marketing and the offering of your items for sale. What are the terms and conditions of the contract and how payment is made or received.

You must ask about reserving bids if the item is of value and you wish to ensure that the items are not sold for less than you feel, or they advise, would be reasonable.

You must ask about the fees for returning the items to you in the event they don't sell. You must enquire about the insuring of your belongings while in their possession in the event of damage or other miscellaneous things.

Weigh all the factors, fees, and conditions prior to committing to an auction of your belongings.

Some examples of auction houses to preview online are:

- Sothebys.
- Christies.
- Bonhams.
- Fellows.
- eBay.

## 8. Estate Sales

An estate sale is a liquidation or sale by auction that is conducted to sell everything or substantially everything of a property often from its location. Estate sales are larger than garage sales and often conducted as a result of a move or to dispose of all the belongings in a deceased estate. They are advertised publicly and may be managed and administered by a professional who has experience in value, pricing and post sale disposition of property. There is a fee or a commission. Dates and times are advertised and the premises is open to the general public for viewing and to purchase. Permits may be required due to factors such as a wide attraction and attendance by the public. There are specified admittance procedures, including signing in to view property.

Estate Sales can be conducted year round.

## 9. Yard and Garage Sales

Yard and garden sales are informal ways to sell items from the premises. Signs are put up around neighborhood, and local notices put in papers or online advising of dates and times. The items are placed out for viewing in garages, under tents, on lawns, tables and any other creative way to show them. Prices are often negotiable. People arrive, look at the items, make offers to purchase and take them away. The homeowner is tasked with setting up the sale and for cleaning up after the sale is over, often donating left items to various organizations. Often people have yard and garage sales for a few weeks prior to moving in hopes of selling as many items as possible before a downsize. Spring, summer and fall are conducive to most yard and garage sales.

Be creative in advertising and showcasing your things. Make them look good. Spruce them up.

If you are staging an open house or a garage sale, you can have tables set aside with a sign "great for upcycling" or "great for repurposing."

For example, instead of a box of buttons, put several of the same color, or size or shape into a baggie with a price suggestion. The same idea for tools, screws in one bag, nails of like sizes in another.

This way items are easy to see, and you tend to get more money for them as they are broken down into smaller take away quantities. If they do not sell, they are neatly packaged for give away.

To save on time, you may want to have tables or areas set up with one big sign at each as opposed to pricing each item.

## 10. Consignment

Consignment is giving your belongings to another to sell, but retaining ownership, subject to contractual terms and conditions, and Consignment Shops (second hand shops) facilitate this. Belongings are brought in, priced, accounted for and an agreement to offer the items for sale to the general public is made between the owner of the property and the consignment operator. The items are placed on display for an agreed upon time period, and when sold, a fee is kept by the consignee. The consignor normally assumes risk associated with the sale of the goods. If the items are not sold as agreed, the items are picked up. In a downsizing scenario, items of good quality can be brought to a consignment store and for a fee, the items will be promoted and displayed and sold.

## 11. Online Selling

Online sales is a very large and growing way to advertise items for sale. If you look under items for sale online, many locations and sites will be presented for your viewing. Online sales will exhibit pictures or very detailed descriptions of the items. Most locations are free to advertise, and some will promote your item for a fee. Sellers need to register by completing a questionnaire indicating their name and other details which may or may not be shown as desired. With online sales, advertisements can be changed and pictures can be added or modified. The interested parties will contact the seller through the website and offers can be made and accepted. The seller will disclose shipping arrangements and set the terms for the payment of shipping. Sales can be via credit card, money order or transfer or using Pay Pal and similar arrangements, which for a fee facilitates the transfer of payment upon notification of receipt of goods. Readers can view eBay, Kijiji for an example of how items are categorized and advertised.

## 12. Buy and Sell and Classifieds

Newspapers have buy and sell sections in their classifieds. Some newspapers are dedicated exclusively to buy and sell, such as car and truck sales. Buy and sell are also features of online offerings to sell an item and an avenue for people looking to purchase items. A picture does not always accompany the advertisement, but a description will. Some buy and sell listings are free, and some carry a fee. They are categorized by subject. The purchaser will contact the seller and negotiations to purchase are made and accepted accordingly. The manner and means of transporting the goods are between buyer and seller.

A sample of a buy and sell ad is sometimes headed by the word "used" "for sale" or "wanted."

## 13. Old Things, New Life

If you have watched *Antiques Roadshow* programs or *Storage Wars*, you have an idea how the reselling of old things has become big business, and how some of the belongings currently being downsized are being sought by collectors and individuals with a desire to acquire.

There is value in well-made goods but not everything that is old is valuable. If the belonging has been well maintained and is in good condition, was built to last, and has markings of identification, such as signatures or stamps, and is rare, a higher value may be given by a collector. Having old things appraised before selling them may be prudent step, before putting them into a yard sale because you are tired of seeing them or because they are no longer in style.

Research: Spend some time looking in arts and crafts shops, and go online to see creative ways some things are being repurposed and used. Do not underestimate the value of nostalgia and what people collect.

Before you discard of something old or broken, or if you are not up to date with the collectible appeal of antiques or retro-era items(1950s and up to about the 1970s) take the time to look at what people are seeking and ask experts their opinions on the appeal of your belongings. Do you have retro jewelry, art, fashion, or even retro games in dusty boxes in your garage or attic? Does your caregiver realize how in-demand and valuable this can be to a collector?

Another reason to perform an inventory in which you label the items you have in your possession is to ensure that something of value is not discarded in error, or overlooked in ignorance.

Repurposing: Creative people are always seeking 'new used goods. The websites Pinterest and Etsy, for example showcase crafts made from discarded items and is well worth having a browse under the heading of crafts.

Older costume jewelry, even the collection of 'one earrings' from a jewelry box or old brooches are highly sought in the world of the crafty and the creative because of their quality craftsmanship, rare metals or unique settings and artistic appeal.

Recycle crayons into collage art works. Remove labels and papers, melt in the oven in muffin tins. They make new shapes and new colors if mixed. You can visit second hand stores and purchase metal cookie shapes and do the same. Pens can be disassembled and refashioned into artistic items.

Socks make great puppets and dusters, and socks hand made from wool and fabric from former days add a value in uniqueness. One sock can make one puppet, mix matched socks can become bracelets or draft blocks for windows and doors.

Computer parts make very interesting works of art that can be assembled, glued onto wood, spray painted and hung.

CDs make beautiful sun catchers.

Old sweaters make wonderful cushion covers.

The list is only as limited as your imagination or the imagination of a creative individual.

7

# Service Providers, Caregivers, and Advisors

The following is a list of professional advisors and other caregivers from whom you are encouraged to obtain guidance and advice as you proceed on your downsizing mission.

- Lawyer.
- Accountant.
- Financial Advisor.
- Physician.
- Counselor.
- Veterinarian.
- Banker.
- Spiritual advisor.
- Community support worker.
- Realtor.
- Home insurer.

- Caregiver.
- Other downsizing service providers as needed.
- Self.

If you are a caregiver or service provider, do you have in hand:

- Agreement to perform services?
- Power of attorney?
- Living will?
- Representation agreement?
- Promissory notes or guarantees to honor?
- Copies of loans or loans secured with personal collateral?
- Copies of lease or rental agreements?
- Any other authority or restriction?
- Any approvals or witnesses required for you to act for yourself?
- Other?

Under what authority are you engaged? What triggered your engagement

What are your responsibilities?

Fill out the questionnaires available on the download kit that came with this book entitled For the Caregiver: What to Look for When Accepting a Downsizing Task, and For Service Providers or Caregivers: Know the Individual or Client.

## 11. Caregivers, Friends, and Family

Caregivers can be professionally trained individuals contracted by health officials to provide services to individuals, patients, or persons of the general public. They can be privately hired individuals who are being paid, or they can be friends, family, neighbors, and acquaintances who assist in the care and well-being of another, often for no compensation. They regularly look after an individual who is sick, frail, disabled, or they might act as companions for the elderly.

Caregivers do many things. Their tasks may include everything from helping an individual in a day-to-day routine such as getting dressed, taking him or her to medical appointments, helping to administer medications, attending doctor's appointments, arranging schedules, grocery shopping, banking, retrieving mail, preparing food, and providing other necessities and assistance.

They are a comforting and reassuring presence to those in need and to the families of those in their care. They assist an individual in making life as comfortable and healthy as possible.

Caregivers listen and attend to the needs of the individual. They are front line in the day-to-day living of an individual and are crucial to communicating with families and health officials.

Caregivers require empathy, patience, communication, and observation skills in sometimes very difficult situations. Caregivers can be live-in individuals, or individuals that attend daily, or on another set or relaxed schedule. For volunteer caregivers, the time they give can exhaust their own energies and resources and they may themselves require respite and assistance.

When an individual that has been cared for is facing a downsizing situation, such as being admitted to a care facility for more intensive care, they may be integral in the planning and carrying out of many or all of their downsizing tasks.

For some individuals, caregiving is a career. For the fortunate caregivers who receive adequate training, a downsizing project may not be a challenge. What could pose a challenge, however, is that aspects of downsizing may not be in the job description. Knowing to whom to delegate in those instances is important.

If individuals who have been providing caregiving services as a volunteer, e.g., for a friend or family member, require help, they can use their knowledge of the individual to secure the services of a downsize company or individual and oversee the process. They can help keep the person calm and involved while sorting and packing and disposing processes are underway and be the go-between, communicating their client, friend, or family member's needs and requests.

If the caregiver completes some of the forms in this guide, such as the Know Yourself questionnaire from Chapter 4 as well as what to look for in securing an downsizing company which was covered in this chapter, they may be equipped to make the transition a smoother and less stressful situation, and it will assist them in making decisions about property issues.

# Download Kit

Please enter the URL you see in the box below into your computer web browser to access and download the kit.

| |
|---|
| www.self-counsel.com/updates/downsizing/14kit.htm |

The kit includes the following:

- Several chapters on other dowsizing issues and solutions.
- Questionnaires on many downsizing issues.